A POCKET GUIDE TO . . .

Compromise

Refuting non-biblical interpretations of Genesis 1

Petersburg, Kentucky, USA

Reprinted August 2017

ISBN: 978-1-60092-422-4

Printed in China

AnswersInGenesis.org

Compromise

Refuting non-biblical interpretations of Genesis 1

WHAT ABOUT THE GAP & RUIN-RECONSTRUCTION THEORIES? • WHAT'S WRONG WITH PROGRESSIVE CREATION? • COULD GOD REALLY HAVE CREATED EVERYTHING IN SIX DAYS? • TEN DANGERS OF THEISTIC EVOLUTION • WHY SHOULDN'T CHRISTIANS ACCEPT MILLIONS OF YEARS?

Table of Contents

Introduction

In order to accommodate supposed long geological ages, many in the church have abandoned the historical understanding of the creation account in Genesis—that God created the entire universe in the space of six normal-length days, roughly 6,000 years ago. Instead, many have invented ideas that are forced upon Scripture, such as the day-age view, gap theory, local flood view, framework hypothesis, theistic evolution, and progressive creation.

Many Christians say that the length of the creation days and the age of the earth are unimportant and divisive side issues that hinder the proclamation of the gospel. But is this really the case?

As you read this pocket guide, you will see that what is at stake is nothing less than the authority of Scripture, the character of God, the doctrine of death, and the very foundation of the gospel. If the early chapters of Genesis are not true literal history, then faith in the rest of the Bible is undermined, including its teaching about salvation and morality.

What About the Gap & Ruin-Reconstruction Theories?

by Ken Ham

Because of the accepted teachings of evolution, many Christians have tried to place a gap of indeterminate time between the first two verses of Genesis 1. Genesis 1:1–2 states: "In the beginning God created the heavens and the earth. The earth was without form, and void; and darkness was on the face of the deep. And the Spirit of God was hovering over the face of the waters."

There are many different versions as to what supposedly happened during this gap of time, but most versions of the gap theory place millions of years of geologic time (including billions of animal

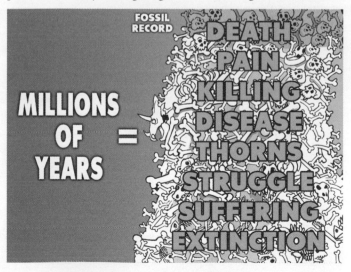

FOSSIL RECORD

MILLIONS OF YEARS = DEATH PAIN KILLING DISEASE THORNS STRUGGLE SUFFERING EXTINCTION

fossils) between the Bible's first two verses. This version of the gap theory is sometimes called the ruin-reconstruction theory.

Most ruin-reconstruction theorists have allowed the fallible theories of secular scientists to determine the meaning of Scripture and have, therefore, accepted the millions-of-years dates for the fossil record.

Some theorists also put the fall of Satan in this supposed period. But any rebellion of Satan during this gap of time contradicts God's description of His completed creation on Day 6 as all being "very good" (Genesis 1:31).

All versions of the gap theory impose outside ideas on Scripture and thus open the door for further compromise.

Where did the gap theory come from?

Christians have made many attempts over the years to harmonize the Genesis account of creation with accepted geology and its teaching of billions of years for the age of the earth. Examples of such attempts include the views of theistic evolution, progressive creation, and the gap theory.

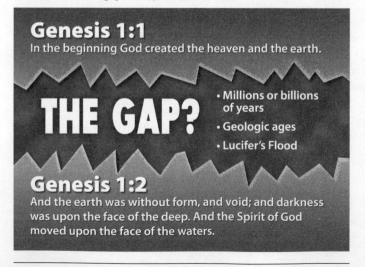

Genesis 1:1
In the beginning God created the heaven and the earth.

THE GAP?
• Millions or billions of years
• Geologic ages
• Lucifer's Flood

Genesis 1:2
And the earth was without form, and void; and darkness was upon the face of the deep. And the Spirit of God moved upon the face of the waters.

This idea of the gap theory can be traced back to the rather obscure writings of the Dutchman Episcopius (1583–1643), but it was first recorded from one of the lectures of Thomas Chalmers.[1] Chalmers (1780–1847) was a notable Scottish theologian and the first moderator of the Free Church of Scotland, and he was perhaps the man most responsible for the gap theory.[2] Rev. William Buckland, a geologist, also did much to popularize the idea.

Although Chalmers' writings give very little information about the gap theory,[3] many of the details are obtained from other writers, such as the nineteenth century geologist Hugh Miller, who quoted from Chalmers' lectures on the subject.[4]

The most notably influential nineteenth century writer to popularize this view was G. H. Pember, in his book *Earth's Earliest Ages*,[5] first published in 1884. Numerous editions of this work were published, the 15th edition appearing in 1942.[6]

The twentieth-century writer who published the most academic defense of the gap theory was Arthur C. Custance in his work *Without Form and Void*.[7]

Bible study aids such as the Scofield Reference Bible, Dake's Annotated Reference Bible, and The Newberry Reference Bible also include the gap theory and have influenced many to accept this teaching. The basic reason for developing and promoting this view can be seen from the following very telling quotes:

Scofield Study Bible: "Relegate fossils to the primitive creation, and no conflict of science with the Genesis cosmogony remains."[8]

Dake's Annotated Reference Bible: "When men finally agree on the age of the earth, then place the many years (over the historical 6,000) between Genesis 1:1 and 1:2, there will be no conflict between the Book of Genesis and science."[9]

These quotes are typical of the many compromise positions—accepting so-called "science"[10] and its long ages for the earth, and incorporating them into Scripture.

A testimony of struggle

G. H. Pember's struggle with long geologic ages, recounted in *Earth's Earliest Ages*, has been the struggle of many Christians ever since the idea of millions of years for the fossil record became popular in the early nineteenth century. Many respected Christian leaders of today wrestle with this same issue.

Reading Pember's struggle helps us understand the implications of the gap theory. Pember, like today's conservative Christians, defended the authority of Scripture. He was adamant that one had to start from Scripture alone and not bring preconceived ideas to Scripture. He boldly chastened people who came to the Bible "filled with myths, philosophies, and prejudices, which they could not altogether throw off, but retained, in part at least, and mingled—quite unwillingly, perhaps—with the truth of God" (p. 5). He describes how the church is weakened when man's philosophies are used to interpret God's Word: "For, by skillfully blending their own systems with the truths of Scripture, they so bewildered the minds of the multitude that but few retained the power of distinguishing the revelation of God from the craftily interwoven teachings of men" (p. 7). He also said, "And the result is that inconsistent and unsound interpretations have been handed down from generation to generation, and received as if they were integral parts of the Scriptures themselves; while any texts which seemed violently opposed were allegorized, spiritualized, or explained away, till they ceased to be troublesome, or perchance, were even made subservient" (p. 8).

He then warns Christians, "For, if we be observant and honest, we must often ourselves feel the difficulty of approaching the sacred writings without bias, seeing that we bring with us a number of stereotyped ideas, which we have received as absolutely certain, and never think of testing, but only seek to confirm" (p. 8).

What happened to Pember should warn us that no matter how great a theologian we may be or how respected and knowledgeable a Christian leader, we, as finite, sinful human beings, cannot easily empty ourselves of preconceived ideas. Pember did exactly what he preached against, without realizing it. Such is the ingrained nature of the long-ages issue. He did not want to question Scripture (he accepted the six literal days of creation), but he did not question the long ages, either. So Pember struggled with what to do. Many of today's respected Christian leaders show the same struggle in their commentaries as they then capitulate to progressive creation or even theistic evolution.[11]

Pember said, "For, as the fossil remains clearly show not only were disease and death—inseparable companions of sin—then prevalent among the living creatures of the earth, but even ferocity and slaughter." He, therefore, recognized that a fossil record of death, decay, and disease before sin was totally inconsistent with the Bible's teaching. And he understood that there could be no carnivores before sin: "On the Sixth Day God pronounced every thing which He had made to be very good, a declaration which would seem altogether inconsistent with the present condition of the animal as well as the vegetable kingdom. Again: He gave the green herb alone for food 'to every beast of the field, and to every fowl of the air, and to every thing that creepeth upon the earth.' There were, therefore, no carnivora in the sinless world" (p. 35).

Pember taught from Isaiah that the earth will be restored to what it was like at first—no more death, disease, or carnivorous activity. However, because he had accepted the long ages for the fossil record, what was he to do with all this death, disease, and destruction in the record? He responded, "Since, then, the fossil remains are those of creatures anterior to Adam, and yet show evident tokens of disease, death, and mutual destruction, they must have belonged to another world, and have a sin-stained history of their own" (p. 35).

Thus, in trying to reconcile the long ages with Scripture, Pember justified the gap theory by saying, "There is room for any length of time between the first and second verses of the Bible. And again; since we have no inspired account of geological formations, we are at liberty to believe that they were developed just in the order which we find them. The whole process took place in pre-Adamite times, in connection, perhaps, with another race of beings, and, consequently, does not at present concern us" (p. 28).

With this background, let us consider this gap theory in detail. Basically, this theory incorporates three strands of thought:

1. A literal view of Genesis.

2. Belief in an extremely long but unidentified age for the earth.

3. An obligation to fit the origin of most of the geologic strata and other geologic evidence between Genesis 1:1 and 1:2. (Gap theorists oppose evolution but believe in an ancient origin of the universe.)

There are many variations of the gap theory. According to the author Weston Fields, the theory can be summarized as follows, "In the far distant dateless past, God created a perfect heaven and perfect earth. Satan was ruler of the earth which was peopled by a race of 'men' without any souls. Eventually, Satan, who dwelled in a garden of Eden composed of minerals (Ezekiel 28), rebelled by desiring to become like God (Isaiah 14). Because of Satan's fall, sin entered the universe and brought on the earth God's judgment in the form of a flood (indicated by the water of 1:2), and then a global ice age when the light and heat from the sun were somehow removed. All the plant, animal, and human fossils upon the earth today date from this 'Lucifer's flood' and do not bear any genetic relationship with the plants, animals, and fossils living upon the earth today."[12]

Some versions of the gap theory state that the fossil record (geologic column) formed over millions of years, and then God destroyed the earth with a catastrophe (i.e., Lucifer's flood) that left it "without form and void."

Western Bible commentaries written before the eighteenth century (before the belief in a long age for the earth became popular) knew nothing of any gap between Genesis 1:1 and 1:2. Certainly some commentaries proposed intervals of various lengths of time for reasons relating to Satan's fall,[13] but none proposed a ruin-reconstruction situation or a pre-Adamite world. In the nineteenth century, it became popular to believe that the geological changes occurred slowly and roughly at the present rate (uniformitarianism[14]). With increased acceptance of uniformitarianism, many theologians urged reinterpretation of Genesis (with ideas such as day-age, progressive creation, theistic evolution, and days-of-revelation).

Problems with the gap theory

Believing in the gap theory presents a number of problems and inconsistencies, especially for a Christian.

1. It is inconsistent with God creating *everything* in six days, as Scripture states.

    Exodus 20:11 says, "For in six days the Lord made the heavens and earth, the sea, and all that is in them, and rested the seventh day. Therefore the Lord blessed the Sabbath day, and hallowed it." Thus the creation of the heavens and the earth (Genesis 1:1) and the sea and all that is in them (the rest of the creation) was completed in six days.[15] Is there any time for a gap?

2. It puts death, disease, and suffering before the Fall, contrary to Scripture.

    Romans 5:12 says, "Therefore, just as through one man [Adam] sin entered the world, and death through sin, and thus death spread to all men, because all sinned." From this we understand that there could not have been human sin or death before Adam. The Bible teaches in 1 Corinthians 15 that

Adam was the first man, and as a result of his rebellion (sin), death and corruption (disease, bloodshed, and suffering) entered the universe. Before Adam sinned, there could not have been any animal (*nephesh*[16]) or human death. Note also that there could not have been a race of men before Adam that died in Lucifer's flood because 1 Corinthians 15:45 tells us that Adam was the first man.

Genesis 1:29–30 teaches us that animals and man were originally created to eat plants, which is consistent with God's description of His creation as "very good." But how could a fossil record, which gives evidence of disease, violence, death, and decay (fossils have been found of animals apparently fighting and certainly eating each other), be described as "very good"? For this to be true, the death of billions of animals (and many humans) as seen in the fossil record must have occurred *after* Adam's sin. The historical event of the global Flood, recorded in Genesis, explains the presence of huge numbers of dead animals buried in rock layers, laid down by water all over the earth.

Romans 8:22 teaches that "the whole creation groans and travails in pain together until now." Clearly the whole of creation was, and is, subject to decay and corruption because of sin. When gap theorists believe that disease, decay, and death existed before Adam sinned, they ignore that this contradicts the teaching of Scripture.[17]

The version of the gap theory that puts Satan's fall at the end of the geological ages, just before the supposed Lucifer's flood that destroyed all pre-Adamic life, has a further problem—the death and suffering recorded in the fossils must have been God's fault. Since it happened before Satan's fall, Satan and sin cannot be blamed for it.[18]

3. The gap theory is logically inconsistent because it explains away what it is supposed to accommodate—supposed evidence for an old earth.

Gap theorists accept that the earth is very old—a belief based on geologic evidence interpreted with the assumption that the present is the key to the past. This assumption implies that in the past sediments containing fossils formed at basically the same rate as they do today. This process is also used by most geologists and biologists to justify belief that the geologic column represents billions of years of earth history. This geologic column has become the showcase of evolution because the fossils are claimed to show ascent from simple to complex life-forms.

This places gap theorists in a dilemma. Committed to literal creation because of their acceptance of a literal view of Genesis, they cannot accept the conclusions of evolution based on the geologic column. Nor can they accept that the days in the Genesis record correspond to geologic periods. So they propose that God reshaped the earth and re-created all life in six literal days after Lucifer's flood (which produced the fossils); hence the name "ruin-reconstruction." Satan's sin supposedly caused this flood, and the resulting judgment upon that sin reduced the previous world to a state of being "without form and void."

While the gap theorist may think Lucifer's flood solves the problem of life before God's creation recorded in Genesis 1:2 and following, this actually removes the reason for the theory in the first place. If all, or most, of the sediments and fossils were produced quickly in one massive worldwide Lucifer's flood, then the main evidence that the earth is extremely old no longer exists, because the age of the earth is based on the assumed slow formation of earth's sediments.

Also, if the world was reduced to a shapeless, chaotic mess, as gap theorists propose, how could a reasonably ordered assemblage of fossils and sediments remain as evidence? Surely with such chaos the fossil record would have been severely disrupted, if not entirely destroyed. This argument also applies to those who say the fossil record formed over hundreds of millions of years before this so-called Lucifer's flood, which would have severely rearranged things.

4. The gap theory does away with the evidence for the historical event of the global Flood.

If the fossil record was formed by Lucifer's flood, then what did the global Flood of Noah's day do? On this point the gap theorist is forced to conclude that the global Flood must have left virtually no trace. To be consistent, the gap theorist would also have to defend that the global Flood was a local event. Custance, one of the major proponents of the gap theory, did just that, and he even published a paper defending a local flood.[19]

Genesis, however, depicts the global Flood as a judgment for man's sin (Genesis 6). Water flooded the earth for over a year (Genesis 6:17, 7:19–24) and only eight people, along with two of every kind (and seven of some) of air-breathing, land-dwelling animal survived (Genesis 7:23). It is more consistent with the whole framework of Scripture to attribute most fossils to the global Flood of Noah's day rather than to resort to a strained interpretation of the fall of Satan[20] and a totally speculative catastrophe that contributes nothing to biblical understanding or to science.

Sadly, in relegating the fossil record to the supposed gap, gappists have removed the evidence of God's judgment in the Flood, which is the basis for God's warning of judgment to come (2 Peter 3:2–14).

5. The gap theorist ignores the evidence for a young earth.

The true gap theorist also ignores evidence consistent with an earth fewer than 10,000 years of age. There is much evidence for this—the decay and rapid reversals of the earth's magnetic field, the amount of salt in the oceans, the wind-up of spiral galaxies, and much more.[21]

6. The gap theory fails to accommodate standard uniformitarian geology with its long ages.

   Today's uniformitarian geologists allow for no worldwide flood of any kind—the imaginary Lucifer's flood or the historical Flood of Noah's day. They also recognize no break between the supposed former created world and the current recreated world.

7. Most importantly, the gap theory undermines the gospel at its foundations.

   By accepting an ancient age for the earth (based on the standard uniformitarian interpretation of the geologic column), gap theorists leave the evolutionary system intact (which by their own assumptions they oppose).

   Even worse, they must also theorize that Romans 5:12 and Genesis 3:3 refer only to spiritual death. But this contradicts other scriptures, such as 1 Corinthians 15 and Genesis 3:22–23. These passages tell us that Adam's sin led to *physical* death, as well as spiritual death. In 1 Corinthians 15 the death of the Last Adam (the Lord Jesus Christ) is compared with the death of the first Adam. Jesus suffered physical death for man's sin, because Adam, the first man, died physically because of sin.

   In cursing man with physical death, God also provided a way to redeem man through the person of His Son Jesus Christ, who suffered the curse of death on the Cross for us. He tasted "death for everyone" according to Hebrews 2:9. He took the penalty that should rightly have been ours at the hands of the Righteous Judge, and bore it in His own body on the Cross. Jesus Christ tasted death for all mankind, and He defeated death when He rose from the grave three days later. Men can be free from eternal death in hell if they believe in Jesus Christ as Lord and Savior. They then are received back to God to spend eternity with Him. That is the message of Christianity.

To believe there was death before Adam's sin destroys the basis of the Christian message. The Bible states that man's rebellious actions led to death and the corruption of the universe, but the gap theory undermines the reason that man needs a Savior.

A closer look at Genesis 1:1–2

The earliest available manuscript of Genesis 1:1–2 is found in the Greek translation of the Old Testament, called the Septuagint (LXX), which was prepared about 250–200 B.C. The LXX does not permit the reading of any ruin-reconstruction scenario into these verses, as even Custance admitted. A closer look at these verses reveals that the gap theory imposes an interpretation upon Genesis 1:1–2 that is unnatural and grammatically unsound. Like many attempts to harmonize the Bible with uniformitarian geology, the gap theory involves a well-meant but misguided twisting of Scripture.

Below are the five major challenges to the gap theory in interpreting Scripture. For a much fuller analysis, we recommend the book *Unformed and Unfilled* by Weston Fields, published by Burgener Enterprises, 1997.

Creating and making (Hebrew: *bara* and *asah*)

It is generally acknowledged that the Hebrew word *bara*, used with "God" as its subject, means "to create"—in the sense of the production of something which did not exist before.

However, according to Exodus 20:11, God "made" (*asah*) the heavens and the earth and everything in them in six days. If God made everything in six days, then there is clearly no room for a gap.

To avoid this clear scriptural testimony against any gap, gap theorists have alleged that *asah* does not mean "to create," but "to form" or even "re-form." They claim that Exodus 20:11 refers not to six days of creation but to six days of re-forming a ruined world.

Is there such a difference between *bara* and *asah* in biblical usage? A number of verses show that, while *asah* may mean "to do" or "to make," it can also mean "to create," which is the same as *bara*. For example,Nehemiah 9:6 states that God made (*asah*) "heaven, the heaven of heavens, with all their host, the earth and everything on it, the seas and all that is in them." This reference is obviously to the original *ex nihilo* (out of nothing) creation, but the word *asah* is used. (We may safely assume that no gappist will want to say that Nehemiah 9:6 refers to the supposed reconstruction, because if the passage did, the gappist would have to include the geological strata in the reconstruction, thereby depriving the whole theory of any power to explain away the fossil record.)

The fact is that the words *bara* and *asah* are often used interchangeably in the Old Testament; indeed, in some places they are used in synonymous parallelism (e.g., Genesis 1:26–27, 2:4; Exodus 34:10; Isaiah 41:20, 43:7).

Applying this conclusion to Exodus 20:11, 31:17, and Nehemiah 9:6, we see that Scripture teaches that God created the universe (everything) in six days, as outlined in Genesis 1.

The grammar of Genesis 1:1–2

Many adherents of the gap theory claim that the grammar of Genesis 1:1–2 allows, and even requires, a time-gap between the events in verse clauses (i.e., three statements that further describe the circumstances introduced by the principal clause in verse 1).

This conclusion is reinforced by the grammarian Gesenius. He says that the Hebrew conjunction *waw*, meaning "and" at the beginning of verse 2, is a "waw copulative," which compares with the old English expression "to wit." This grammatical connection between verses 1 and 2 thus rules out the gap theory. Verse 2 is in fact a description of the state of the originally created earth: "And the earth was without form and void" (Genesis 1:2a).[22]

"Was" or "became"?

Gappists translate "the earth *was* without form and void" to be "the earth *became* (or, *had become*) without form and void." At stake is the translation of the Hebrew word *hayetah* (a form of the Hebrew verb, *hayah*, meaning "to be").

Custance, a supporter of the gap theory, claims that out of 1,320 occurrences of the verb *hayah* in the Old Testament, only 24 can certainly be said to bear the meaning "to be." He concludes that in Genesis 1:2 *hayetah* must mean "became" and not simply "was."

However, we must note that the meaning of a word is controlled by its context, and that verse 2 is circumstantial to verse 1. Thus "was" is the most natural and appropriate translation for *hayetah*. It is rendered this way in most English versions (as well as in the LXX). Furthermore, in Genesis 1:2 *hayetah* is not followed by the preposition *le*, which would have removed any ambiguity in the Hebrew and required the translation "became."

Tohu and *bohu*

The words *tohu* and *bohu*, usually translated "formless and void," are used in Genesis 1:2. They imply that the original universe was created unformed and unfilled and was, during six days, formed and filled by God's creative actions.

Gappists claim that these words imply a process of judgmental destruction and that they indicate a sinful, and therefore not an original, state of the earth. However, this brings interpretations from other parts of the Old Testament with very different contexts (namely, Isaiah 34:11 and Jeremiah 4:23) and imports them into Genesis 1.

Tohu and *bohu* appear together only in the three above-mentioned places in the Old Testament. However, *tohu* appears alone in a number of other places and in all cases simply means "formless." The word itself does not tell us about the cause of formlessness; this has to be gleaned from the context. Isaiah 45:18 (often quoted by gappists) is rendered in the KJV "he created it not in vain [*tohu*], he formed it to be inhabited." In the context, Isaiah is speaking about Israel, God's people, and His grace in restoring them. He did not choose His people in order to destroy them, but to be their God and for them to be His people. Isaiah draws an analogy with God's purpose in creation: He did not create the world for it to be empty. No, He created it to be formed and filled, a suitable abode for His creation. Gappists miss the point altogether when they argue that because Isaiah says God did not create the world *tohu*, it must have *become tohu* at some later time. Isaiah 45:18 is about God's purpose in creating, not about the original state of the creation.

Though the expression "*tohu* and *bohu*" in Isaiah 34:11 and Jeremiah 4:23 speaks of a formlessness and emptiness resulting from divine judgment for sin, this meaning is not implicit in the expression itself but is gained from the particular contexts in which it occurs. It is not valid therefore to infer that same meaning from Genesis 1:2, where the context does not suggest any judgment. As an analogy, we might think of a word like "blank" in reference to a computer screen. It can be blank because nothing has been typed on the keyboard, or it can be blank because the screen has been erased. The word "blank" does not suggest, in itself, the reason why the screen is blank. Likewise with "formless and void"—the earth began that way simply because it was not yet formed and filled, or it was that way because of judgment.

Theologians call the form of use of *tohu* and/or *bohu* in Isaiah 34:11 and Jeremiah 4:23 a "verbal allusion." These passages on judgment allude to the formless and empty earth at the beginning of creation to suggest the extent of God's judgment to come. God's judgment will be so complete that the result will be like the earth before it was formed and filled—formless and empty. This does not imply that the state of the creation in Genesis 1:2 was arrived at by some sort of judgment or destruction as imagined by gappists. As theologian Robert Chisholm, Jr. wrote, "By the way, allusion only works one way. It is unwarranted to assume that Jeremiah's use of the phrase in a context of judgment implies some sort of judgment in the context of Genesis 1:2. Jeremiah is not interpreting the meaning of Genesis 1:2."[23]

"Replenish"

Many gappists have used the word "replenish" in the KJV translation of Genesis 1:28 to justify the gap theory on the basis that this word means "refill." Thus, they claim that God told Adam and Eve to refill the earth, implying it was once before filled with people (the pre-Adamites). However, this is wrong. The Hebrew word translated "replenish," male,[24] simply means "fill" (or "fulfill" or "be filled").

The English word "replenish" meant "fill" from the thirteenth to the seventeenth centuries; then it changed to mean "refill." When the KJV was published in 1611, the translators used the English word "replenish," which at that time meant only "fill," not "refill."[25]

The straightforward meaning of Genesis 1:1–2

The gap (or ruin-reconstruction) theory is based on a very tenuous interpretation of Scripture.

The simple, straightforward meaning of Genesis 1:1–2 is that, when God created the earth at the beginning, it was initially formless, empty, and dark, and God's Spirit was there above the waters. It was through His creative energy that the world was then progressively formed and filled during the six days of creation.

Consider the analogy of a potter making a vase. The first thing he does is gather a ball of clay. What he has is good, but it is unformed. Next, he shapes it into a vase, using his potter's wheel. Now the ball of clay is no longer formless. He then dries it, applies glaze, and fires it. Now it is ready to be filled—with flowers and water. At no time could one of the stages be considered evil or bad. It was just unfinished—unformed and unfilled. When the vase was finally formed and filled, it could be described as "very good."

Warning

Many sincere Christians have invented reinterpretations of Scripture to avoid intellectual conflicts with popular scientific ideas. The gap theory was one such reinterpretation designed to fit in with scientific concepts that arose in the early 1800s and are still popular today.

In reality, though, the gap theory was an effective anesthetic that put the church to sleep for over 100 years. When the children who learned this compromise position went on to higher education, they were shocked to discover that this theory explained nothing. Many of them then accepted the only remaining "respectable" theory—evolution—which went hand-in-hand with millions of years. The results were usually disastrous for their faith.

Today, other compromise positions, such as progressive creation or theistic evolution, have mostly replaced the gap theory.[26] The gappists, by attempting to maintain a literal Genesis but adhering to the long ages (millions of years), opened the door for greater compromise in the next generation—the reinterpretation of the days, God using evolution, etc.

But whether it is the gap theory, day-age/progressive creation, or theistic evolution, the results are the same. These positions may be acceptable in some churches, but the learned in the secular world will, with some justification, mock those who hold them because they see the inconsistencies.

In Martin Luther's day the church compromised what the Bible clearly taught, and he nailed his *Ninety-Five Theses* to the door of the church to call them back to the authority of God's Word. In the same way, the church today has, by and large, neglected what the Bible clearly says in Genesis 1–11. It's time to call the church back to the authority of God's Word beginning with Genesis.

1.   I. Taylor, *In the Minds of Men: Darwin and the New World Order* (TFE Publishing, 1984), p. 363.

2.   W.W. Fields, *Unformed and Unfilled* (Burgeners Enterprises,1976), p. 40.

3.   W. Hanna, ed., *Natural Theology*, Selected works of Thomas Chalmers, Vol. 5 (Thomas Constable, Edinburgh, 1857), p. 146. The only thing Chalmers basically states concerning the gap theory in these writings is, "The detailed history of creation in the first chapter of Genesis begins at the middle of the second verse."

4.   H. Miller, *The Testimony of the Rocks* (Gould and Lincoln, 1867), p. 143.

5. G.H. Pember, *Earth's Earliest Ages* (H. Revell Company, 1900).

6. Taylor, *In the Minds of Men*, p. 363.

7. A.C. Custance, *Without Form and Void*, 1970.

8. C.I. Scofield, ed., *The Scofield Study Bible* (Oxford University Press, 1945). Originally published as *The Scofield Reference Bible*; this edition is unaltered from the original of 1909.

9. F.H. Dake, *Dake's Annotated Reference Bible* (Dake Bible Sales, 1961), p. 51.

10. Many people now equate the teaching of millions of years and evolution with science. However, these teachings are *not* science in the empirical (repeatable, testable) sense. Scientists have only the present to work with. To connect the present to the past involves interpretations based on unprovable assumptions.

11. K. Ham, "Millions of years and the 'doctrine of Balaam,'" *Creation* 19(3):15–17, 1997.

12. Fields, *Unformed and Unfilled*, p. 7.

13. Those who try to put the fall of Satan (not connected with millions of years) into this gap, need to consider that if all the angels were a part of the original creation, as Exodus 20:11 indicates and Colossians 1 seems to confirm, then *everything* God had created by the end of the sixth day was "very good." There could not have been *any* rebellion before this time. So Satan fell sometime after Day 7.

14. The term "uniformitarian" commonly refers to the idea that geological processes, such as erosion and sedimentation, have remained essentially the same throughout time, and so the present is the key to the past. But after the mid-nineteenth century, the application of the concept has been extended. Huxley said, "Consistent uniformitarianism postulates evolution as much in the organic as in the inorganic world." It is now assumed that a closed system exists, to which neither God nor any other nonhuman or non-natural force has access (from J. Rendle-Short, *Man: Ape or Image* (Master Books, 1984), p. 20, note 4.

15. For more details, see "Could God Really Have Created Everything in Six Days?" page 55.

16. The Bible speaks of animals and humans having or being *nephesh* (Hebrew), or soul-life, in various contexts suggesting conscious life. The death of a jellyfish, for example, may not be death of a *nephesh* animal.

17. See K. Ham, *The Lie: Evolution* (Master Books, 1987), pp. 71–82.

18. H. Morris, "Why the gap theory won't work," *Back to Genesis* No. 107 (Institute for Creation Research, 1997).

19. A.C. Custance, "The Flood: local or global?" *The Doorway Papers* Vol. 9 (Zondervan, 1970).

20. This also impinges upon the perspicuity of Scripture—that is, that the Bible is clear and understandable to ordinary Christians in all that's important.

21. D.R. Humphreys, "Evidence for a young world," *Creation* 13(3):46–50, 1991. See also www.answersingenesis.org/go/young.

22. The word "and" is included in the KJV translation but is translated "now" in the NIV and is not translated at all in the NKJV or the NASB.

23. R.B. Chisholm, Jr., *From Exegesis to Exposition: A Practical Guide to Using Biblical Hebrew* (Baker Books, 1998), p. 41.

24. *Strong's Concordance*, Hebrew word No. 4390.

25. See C. Taylor, "What does 'replenish the earth' mean?" *Creation* 18(2):44–45, 1996, for more details on the history of the meaning of "replenish."

26. A strange modern gap theory is found in *Genesis Unbound*, by J. Sailhamer (Multnomah Books, 1996). The author fits the supposed millions of years of geologic history into Genesis 1:1 and then claims the six days of creation relate to the Promised Land. He states his motivation for this novel approach on p. 29: "If billions of years really are covered by the

simple statement, 'In the beginning God created the heavens and the earth,' then many of the processes described by modern scientists fall into the period covered by the Hebrew term 'beginning.' Within that 'beginning' would fit the countless geologic ages, ice ages, and the many global climatic changes on our planet. The many biological eras would also fit within 'the beginning' of Genesis 1:1, including the long ages during which the dinosaurs roamed the earth. By the time human beings were created on the sixth day of the week, the dinosaurs already could have flourished and become extinct—all during the 'beginning' recorded in Genesis 1:1." Many of the problems with the classical gap theory also apply to this attempt to fit millions of years into the Bible.

Ken Ham is President and CEO of Answers in Genesis–USA and the Creation Museum. Ken's bachelor's degree in applied science (with an emphasis on environmental biology) was awarded by the Queensland Institute of Technology in Australia. He also holds a diploma of education from the University of Queensland. In recognition of the contribution Ken has made to the church in the USA and internationally, Ken has been awarded two honorary doctorates: a Doctor of Divinity (1997) from Temple Baptist College in Cincinnati, Ohio and a Doctor of Literature (2004) from Liberty University in Lynchburg, Virginia.

Ken has authored or co-authored many books concerning the authority and accuracy of God's Word and the effects of evolutionary thinking, including *Genesis of a Legacy* and *The Lie: Evolution*.

Since moving to America in 1987, Ken has become one of the most in-demand Christian conference speakers and talk show guests in America. He has appeared on national shows such as Fox's *The O'Reilly Factor* and *Fox and Friends in the Morning*; CNN's *The Situation Room with Wolf Blitzer*, ABC's *Good Morning America*, the BBC, *CBS News Sunday Morning*, *The NBC Nightly News with Brian Williams*, and *The PBS News Hour with Jim Lehrer*.

What's Wrong with Progressive Creation?

by Ken Ham & Terry Mortenson

One result of compromising with our evolutionary culture is the view of creation called the "day-age" theory or "progressive creation." This view, while not a new one, has received wide publicity in the past several years. Much of this publicity is due to the publications and lectures of astronomer Dr. Hugh Ross—probably the world's leading progressive creationist. Dr. Ross's views on how to interpret the Book of Genesis won early endorsements from many well-known Christian leaders, churches, seminaries, and Christian colleges. The teachings of Dr. Ross seemingly allowed Christians to use the term "creationist" but still gave them supposed academic respectability in the eyes of the world by rejecting six literal days of creation and maintaining billions of years. However, after his views became more fully understood, many who had previously embraced progressive creation realized how bankrupt those views are and removed their endorsement.

In this chapter, some of the teachings of progressive creation will be examined in light of Scripture and good science.[1]

In summary, progressive creation teaches:

- The big-bang origin of the universe occurred about 13–15 billion years ago.

- The days of creation were overlapping periods of millions and billions of years.

- Over millions of years, God created new species as others kept going extinct.

- The record of nature is just as reliable as the Word of God.

- Death, bloodshed, and disease existed before Adam and Eve.

- Manlike creatures that looked and behaved much like us (and painted on cave walls) existed before Adam and Eve but did not have a spirit that was made in the image of God, and thus had no hope of salvation.

- The Genesis Flood was a local event.

The big bang origin of the universe

Progressive creation teaches that the modern big-bang theory of the origin of the universe is true and has been proven by scientific inquiry and observation. For Hugh Ross and others like him, big-bang cosmology becomes the basis by which the Bible is interpreted. This includes belief that the universe and the earth are billions of years old. Dr. Ross even goes so far as to state that life would not be possible on earth without billions of years of earth history:

> It only works in a cosmos of a hundred-billion trillion stars that's precisely sixteen-billion-years old. This is the narrow window of time in which life is possible.[2]

Life is only possible when the universe is between 12 and 17 billion years.[3]

This, of course, ignores the fact that God is omnipotent—He could make a fully functional universe ready for life right from the beginning, for with God nothing is impossible (Matthew 19:26).[4]

The days of creation in Genesis 1

Progressive creationists claim that the days of creation in Genesis 1 represent long periods of time. In fact, Dr. Ross believes day

3 of creation week lasted more than 3 billion years![5] This assertion is made in order to allow for the billions of years that evolutionists claim are represented in the rock layers of earth. This position, however, has problems, both biblically and scientifically.

The text of Genesis 1 clearly states that God supernaturally created all that is in six actual days. If we are prepared to let the words of the text speak to us in accord with the context and their normal definitions, without influence from outside ideas, then the word for "day" in Genesis 1 obviously means an ordinary day of about 24 hours. It is qualified by a number, the phrase "evening and morning," and for day 1, the words "light and darkness."[6]

Dr. James Barr, Regius Professor of Hebrew at Oxford University, who himself does not believe Genesis is true history, admitted the following, as far as the language of Genesis 1 is concerned:

> So far as I know, there is no professor of Hebrew or Old Testament at any world-class university who does not believe that the writer(s) of Gen. 1–11 intended to convey to their readers the ideas that (a) creation took place in a series of six days which were the same as the days of 24 hours we now experience, (b) the figures contained in the Genesis genealogies provided by simple addition a chronology from the beginning of the world up to later stages in the biblical story, (c) Noah's Flood was understood to be world-wide and extinguish all human and animal life except for those in the ark.[7]

Besides the textual problems, progressive creationists have scientific dilemmas as well. They accept modern scientific measurements for the age of the earth, even though these measurements are based on evolutionary, atheistic assumptions. Dr. Ross often speaks of the "facts of nature" and the "facts of science" when referring to the big bang and billions of years. This demonstrates his fundamental misunderstanding of evidence. The scientific "facts" that evolutionists claim as proof of millions of years are really interpretations of selected observations that have been made with antibiblical and usually atheistic, philosophical assumptions. We all have the same facts: the same living creatures, the same DNA molecules, the same fossils, the same rock layers, the same Grand Canyon, the same moon, the same planets, the same starlight from distant stars and galaxies, etc. These are the facts; how old they are and how they formed are the interpretations of the facts. And what one believes about history will affect how one interprets these facts. History is littered with so-called "scientific facts" that supposedly had proven the Bible wrong, but which were shown years or decades later to be not facts but erroneously interpreted observations because of the antibiblical assumptions used.[8]

The order of creation

As their name indicates, progressive creationists believe that God progressively created species on earth over billions of years, with new species replacing extinct ones, starting with simple organisms and culminating in the creation of Adam and Eve. They accept the evolutionary order for the development of life on earth, even though this contradicts the order given in the Genesis account of creation.[9] Evolutionary theory holds that the first life forms were marine organisms, while the Bible says that God created land plants first. Reptiles are supposed to have predated birds,

Progressive Creation

while Genesis says that birds came first. Evolutionists believe that land mammals came before whales, while the Bible teaches that God created whales first.

Dr. Davis Young, emeritus geology professor at Calvin College, recognized this dilemma and abandoned the "day-age" theory. Here is part of his explanation as to why he discarded it:

> The biblical text, for example, has vegetation appearing on the third day and animals on the fifth day. Geology, however, had long realized that invertebrate animals were swarming in the seas long before vegetation gained a foothold on the land. . . . Worse yet, the text states that on the fourth day God made the heavenly bodies after the earth was already in existence. Here is a blatant confrontation with science. Astronomy insists that the sun is older than the earth.[10]

The sixty-seventh book of the Bible

Dr. Ross has stated that he believes nature to be "just as perfect" as the Bible. Here is the full quote:

> Not everyone has been exposed to the sixty-six books of the Bible, but everyone on planet Earth has been exposed to the sixty-seventh book—the book that God has

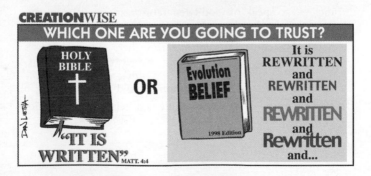

written upon the heavens for everyone to read.

And the Bible tells us it's impossible for God to lie, so the record of nature must be just as perfect, and reliable and truthful as the sixty-six books of the Bible that is part of the Word of God. . . . And so when astronomers tell us [their attempts to measure distance in space] . . . it's part of the truth that God has revealed to us. It actually encompasses part of the Word of God.[3]

Dr. Ross is right that God cannot lie, and God tells us in Romans 8:22 that "the whole creation groans and labors with birth pangs" because of sin. And not only was the universe cursed, but man himself has been affected by the Fall. So how can sinful, fallible human beings in a sin-cursed universe say that their interpretation of the evidence is as perfect as God's written revelation? Scientific assertions must use fallible assumptions and fallen reasoning—how can this be the Word of God?

The respected systematic theologian Louis Berkhof said:

Since the entrance of sin into the world, man can gather true knowledge about God from His general revelation only if he studies it in the light of Scripture, in which the elements of God's original self-revelation, which were obscured and perverted by the blight of sin, are republished, corrected, and interpreted. . . . Some are inclined to speak of God's general revelation as a second source; but this is hardly correct in view of the fact that nature can come into consideration here only as interpreted in the light of Scripture.[11]

In other words, Christians should build their thinking on the Bible, not on fallible interpretations of scientific observations about the past.

Death and disease before Adam

Progressive creationists believe the fossil record was formed from the millions of animals that lived and died before Adam and Eve were created. They accept the idea that there was death, bloodshed, and disease (including cancer) before sin, which goes directly against the teaching of the Bible and dishonors the character of God.

God created a perfect world at the beginning. When He was finished, God stated that His creation was "very good." The Bible makes it clear that man and all the animals were vegetarians before the Fall (Genesis 1:29-30). Plants were given to them for food (plants do not have a *nephesh* [life spirit] as man and animals do and thus eating them would not constitute "death" in the biblical sense[12]).

Concerning the entrance of sin into the world, Dr. Ross writes, "The groaning of creation in anticipation of release from sin has lasted fifteen billion years and affected a hundred billion trillion stars."[13]

However, the Bible teaches something quite different. In the context of human death, the apostle Paul states, "Through one man sin entered the world, and death through sin" (Romans 5:12). It is clear that there was no sin in the world before Adam sinned, and thus no death.

God killed the first animal in the Garden and shed blood because of sin. If there were death, bloodshed, disease, and suffering before sin, then the basis for the atonement is destroyed. Christ suffered death because death was the penalty for sin. There will be no death or suffering in the perfect "restoration"—so why can't we accept the same in a perfect ("very good") creation before sin?

God must be quite incompetent and cruel to make things in the way that evolutionists imagine the universe and earth to have evolved, as most creatures that ever existed died cruel deaths. Progressive creation denigrates the wisdom and goodness of God by suggesting that this was God's method of creation. This view attacks His truthfulness as well. If God really created over the course of billions of years, then He has misled most believers for 4,000 years into believing that He did it in six days.[14]

Spiritless hominids before Adam

Since evolutionary radiometric dating methods have dated certain humanlike fossils as older than Ross's date for modern humans (approx. 40,000 years), he and other progressive creationists insist that these are fossils of pre-Adamic creatures that had no spirit, and thus no salvation.

Dr. Ross accepts and defends these evolutionary dating methods, so he must redefine all evidence of humans (descendants of Noah) if they are given evolutionary dates of more than about 40,000 years (e.g., the Neanderthal cave sites) as related to spiritless "hominids," which the Bible does not mention. However, these same methods have been used to "date" the Australian Aborigines back at least 60,000 years (some have claimed much older) and fossils of "anatomically modern humans" to over 100,000 years.[15] By Ross's reasoning, none of these (including the Australian Aborigines) could be descendants of Adam and Eve. However, Acts 17:26 says, "And He has made from one blood every nation of men to dwell on all the face of the earth, and has determined their preappointed times and the boundaries of their dwellings" (NKJV). All people on earth are descendants of Adam.

In addition, the fossil record cannot, by its very nature, conclusively reveal if a creature had a spirit or not, since spirits are not fossilized. But there is clear evidence that creatures, which Ross (following the evolutionists) places before Adam, had art and

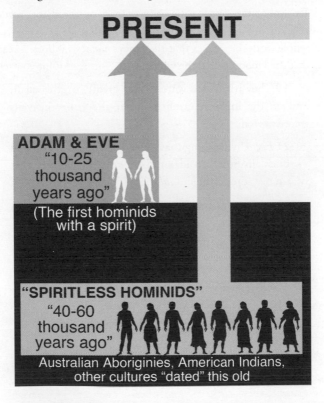

PRESENT

ADAM & EVE
"10-25 thousand years ago"
(The first hominids with a spirit)

"SPIRITLESS HOMINIDS"
"40-60 thousand years ago"
Australian Aboriginies, American Indians, other cultures "dated" this old

clever technology and that they buried their dead in a way that many of Adam's descendants have.[16] Therefore, we have strong reason to believe that they were fully human and actually descendants of Adam, and that they lived only a few thousand years ago.

The Genesis Flood

One important tenet of progressive creation is that the Flood of Noah's day was a local flood, limited to the Mesopotamian region. Progressive creationists believe that the rock layers and fossils found around the world are the result of billions of years of evolutionary earth history, rather than from the biblical Flood.

Dr. Ross often says that he believes in a "universal" or "worldwide" flood, but in reality he does not believe that the Flood covered the whole earth. He argues that the text of Genesis 7 doesn't really say that the Flood covered the whole earth. But read it for yourself:

19 They [the flood waters] rose greatly on the earth, and *all* the high mountains under the *entire* heavens were covered.

21 *Every* living thing that moved on the earth perished — birds, livestock, wild animals, *all* the creatures that swarm over the earth, and *all* mankind.

22 *Everything* on dry land that had the breath of life in its nostrils died.

23 *Every* living thing on the face of the earth was wiped out; men and animals and the creatures that move along

the ground and the birds of the air were wiped from the earth. *Only* Noah was left, and those with him in the ark [emphasis added].

Also, many questions remain for those who teach that the Genesis flood was only local:

- If the Flood was local, why did Noah have to build an ark? He could have walked to the other side of the mountains and missed it.

- If the Flood was local, why did God send the animals to the ark so they could escape death? There would have been other animals to reproduce that kind if these particular ones had died.

- If the Flood was local, why was the ark big enough to hold all the different kinds of vertebrate land animals? If only Mesopotamian animals were aboard, the ark could have been much smaller.[17]

A local flood that rose above the mountains?

- If the Flood was local, why would birds have been sent on board? These could simply have winged across to a nearby mountain range.

- If the Flood was local, how could the waters rise to 15 cubits (8 meters) above the mountains (Genesis 7:20)? Water seeks its own level. It couldn't rise to cover the local mountains while leaving the rest of the world untouched.

- If the Flood was local, people who did not happen to be living in the vicinity would not be affected by it. They would have escaped God's judgment on sin. If this had happened, what did Christ mean when He likened the coming judgment of all men to the judgment of "all" men in the days of Noah (Matthew 24:37–39)? A partial judgment in Noah's day means a partial judgment to come.

- If the Flood was local, God would have repeatedly broken His promise never to send such a flood again.

Conclusion

It is true that whether one believes in six literal days does not ultimately affect one's salvation, if one is truly born again. However, we need to stand back and look at the "big picture." In many nations, the Word of God was once widely respected and taken seriously. But once the door of compromise is unlocked and Christian leaders concede that we shouldn't take the Bible as written in Genesis, why should the world take heed of it in *any* area? Because the Church has told the world that one can use man's interpretation of the world (such as billions of years) to reinterpret the Bible, it is seen as an outdated, scientifically incorrect "holy book," not intended to be taken seriously.

As each subsequent generation has pushed this door of compromise open farther and farther, increasingly they are not accepting the morality or salvation of the Bible either. After all, if the history in Genesis is not correct as written, how can one be sure the rest can be taken as written? Jesus said, "If I have told you earthly things and you do not believe, how will you believe if I tell you heavenly things?" (John 3:12).

It would not be exaggerating to claim that the majority of Christian leaders and laypeople within the church today do not believe in six literal days. Sadly, being influenced by the world has led to the Church no longer powerfully influencing the world.

The "war of the worldviews" is not ultimately one of young earth versus old earth, or billions of years versus six days, or creation versus evolution—the real battle is the authority of the Word of God versus man's fallible theories.

Belief in a historical Genesis is important because progressive creation and its belief in millions of years (1) contradicts the clear teaching of Scripture, (2) assaults the character of God, (3) severely damages and distorts the Bible's teaching on death, and (4) undermines the gospel by undermining the clear teaching of Genesis, which gives the whole basis for Christ's atonement and our need for a Redeemer. So ultimately, the issue of a literal Genesis is about the authority of the Word of God versus the authority of the words of sinful men.

Why do Christians believe in the bodily resurrection of Jesus Christ? Because of the *words of Scripture* ("according to the Scriptures").

And why should Christians believe in six literal days of creation? Because of the *words of Scripture* ("In six days the Lord made . . .").

The real issue is one of authority—let us unashamedly stand upon God's Word as our sole authority!

---

1. For a more complete analysis, see Jonathan Sarfati, *Refuting Compromise* (Master Books, 2004); Tim Chaffey and Jason Lisle, *Old-Earth Creationism on Trial* (Master Books, 2008); Mark Van Bebber and Paul S. Taylor, *Creation and Time: A Report on the Progressive Creation Book by Hugh Ross* (Eden Publications, 1994); http://www.answersingenesis.org/home/area/faq/compromise.asp.

2. Dallas Theological Seminary chapel service, September 13, 1996.

---

3. Toccoa Falls Christian College, Staley Lecture Series, March 1997.

4. For an evaluation of the big bang model, see "Does the Big Bang Fit with the Bible?" in *The New Answers Book 2* (Master Books, 2008),

5. http://www.reasons.org/creation-timeline, September 13, 2005.

6. See "Could God Really Have Created Everything in Six Days" by Ken Ham, page 55, for a more detailed defense of literal days in Genesis 1.

7. Letter to David C.C. Watson, April 23, 1984.

8. For more on how our presuppositions influence our interpretation, see "What's the Best 'Proof' of Creation?" in *The New Answers Book 2* (Master Books, 2008).

9. Answers in Genesis website: "Evolution vs. Creation: The Order of Events Matters!" Dr. Terry Mortenson, April 4, 2006, http://www.answersingenesis.org/docs2006/0404order.asp.

10. D. Young, *The Harmonization of Scripture and Science*, science symposium at Wheaton College, March 23, 1990.

11. L. Berkhof, *Introductory volume to Systematic Theology* (Eerdmans Publ. Co., 1946), pp. 60, 96.

12. For more details, see "How Did Defense/Attack Structures Come About?" by Andy McIntosh and Bodie Hodge in *The New Answers Book 1* (Master Books, 2006).

13. Hugh Ross, "The Physics of Sin," *Facts for Faith*, Issue 8, 2002, http://www.reasons.org/resources/publications/facts-faith/2002issue08#physics_of_sin.

14. Dr. Terry Mortenson, "Genesis According to Evolution," *Creation* 26(4) September 2004: 50–51.

15. T. White et al., "Pleistocene Homo sapiens from Middle Awash, Ethiopia," *Nature* 423 (June 12, 2003): 742–747. Dr. Ross will permit up to 60,000 years, but this is extreme for this position.

16. Marvin Lubelow, *Bones of Contention*, revised and updated (Baker Books, 2004).

17. See John Woodmorappe, *Noah's Ark: A Feasibility Study* (Institute for Creation Research, 1996).

Dr. Terry Mortenson earned a PhD in the history of geology from the University of Coventry in England and an MDiv from Trinity Evangelical Divinity School in Chicago. He has lectured on the creation-evolution controversy in 19 countries since the late 1970s.

Dr. Mortenson is the author of numerous magazine, journal, and web articles, as well as several book chapters. The revised version of his PhD thesis was published as *The Great Turning Point: the Church's Catastrophic Mistake on Geology—Before Darwin*. Dr. Mortenson co-edited and contributed two chapters to the scholarly 14-author book *Coming to Grips with Genesis: Biblical Authority and the Age of the Earth*. Currently he serves as a speaker, researcher, and writer for Answers in Genesis–USA.

Ten Dangers of Theistic Evolution

by Werner Gitt

The atheistic formula for evolution is:

Evolution = matter + evolutionary factors (chance and necessity + mutation + selection + isolation + death) + very long time periods.

In the theistic evolutionary view, God is added:

Theistic evolution = matter + evolutionary factors (chance and necessity + mutation + selection + isolation + death) + very long time periods + God.

What is theistic evolution?

The following evolutionary assumptions are generally applicable to theistic evolution:

- The basic principle, evolution, is taken for granted.

- It is believed that evolution is a universal principle.

- As far as scientific laws are concerned, there is no difference between the origin of the earth and all life and their subsequent development (the principle of uniformity).

- Evolution relies on processes that allow increases in organization from the simple to the complex, from non-life to life, and from lower to higher forms of life.

- The driving forces of evolution are mutation, selection, isolation, and mixing. Chance and necessity, long time epochs, ecological changes, and death are additional indispensable factors.

- The time line is so prolonged that anyone can have as much time as he/she likes for the process of evolution.

- The present is the key to the past.

- There was a smooth transition from non-life to life.

- Evolution will persist into the distant future.

In addition to these evolutionary assumptions, three additional beliefs apply to theistic evolution:

1. God used evolution as a means of creating.

2. The Bible contains no usable or relevant ideas which can be applied in present-day origins science.

3. Evolutionistic pronouncements have priority over biblical statements. The Bible must be reinterpreted when and wherever it contradicts the present evolutionary worldview.

In this system God is not the omnipotent Lord of all things, who's Word has to be taken seriously by all men, but He is integrated into the evolutionary philosophy. This leads to 10 dangers for Christians.[1]

Danger no. 1: Misrepresentation of the nature of God

The Bible reveals God to us as our Father in Heaven, who is absolutely perfect (Matthew 5:48), holy (Isaiah 6:3), and omnipotent (Jeremiah 32:17). The Apostle John tells us that God is love, light, and life (1 John 4:16; 1:5; 1:1–2). When this God creates something, His work is described as "very good" (Genesis 1:31) and "perfect" (Deuteronomy 32:4).

Theistic evolution gives a false representation of the nature of God because death and ghastliness are ascribed to the Creator as principles of creation.

Danger no. 2: God becomes a God of the gaps

The Bible states that God is the Prime Cause of all things. "Yet for us there is one God, the Father, of whom are all things . . . and one Lord Jesus Christ, through whom are all things." (1 Corinthians 8:6).

However, in theistic evolution the only workspace allotted to God is that part of nature which evolution cannot "explain" with the means presently at its disposal. In this way He is reduced to being a "god of the gaps" for those phenomena about which there are doubts. This leads to the view that "God is therefore not absolute, but He Himself has evolved—He is evolution."[2]

Danger no. 3: Denial of central biblical teachings

The entire Bible bears witness that we are dealing with a source of truth authored by God (2 Timothy 3:16), with the Old Testament as the indispensable "ramp" leading to the New Testament, like an access road leads to a motor freeway (John 5:39). The biblical creation account should not be regarded as a myth, a parable, or an allegory, but as a historical report, because:

- Biological, astronomical, and anthropological facts are given in didactic [teaching] form.

- In the Ten Commandments God bases the six working days and one day of rest on the same time-span as that described in the creation account (Exodus 20:8–11).

- In the New Testament Jesus referred to facts of the creation (e.g. Matthew 19:4–5).

- Nowhere in the Bible are there any indications that the creation account should be understood in any other way than as a factual report.

The doctrine of theistic evolution undermines this basic way of reading the Bible, as vouched for by Jesus, the prophets, and the apostles. Events reported in the Bible are reduced to mythical imagery, and an understanding of the message of the Bible as being true in word and meaning is lost.

Danger no. 4: Loss of the way for finding God

The Bible describes man as being completely ensnared by sin after Adam's fall (Romans 7:18–19). Only those persons who realize that they are sinful and lost will seek the Savior who came "to seek and to save that which was lost" (Luke 19:10).

However, evolution knows no sin in the biblical sense of missing one's purpose (in relation to God). Sin is made meaningless, and that is exactly the opposite of what the Holy Spirit does—He declares sin to be sinful. If sin is seen as a harmless evolutionary factor, then one has lost the key for finding God, which is not resolved by adding "God" to the evolutionary scenario.

Danger no. 5: The doctrine of God's incarnation is undermined

The incarnation of God through His Son Jesus Christ is one of the basic teachings of the Bible. The Bible states that "the Word became flesh and dwelt among us" (John 1:14) and that Jesus Christ came "in the likeness of men" (Philippians 2:7).[3]

Danger no. 6: The biblical basis of Jesus's work of redemption is mythologized

The Bible teaches that the first man's fall into sin was a real event and that this was the direct cause of sin in the world. "Therefore, just as through one man sin entered the world, and death through sin, and thus death spread to all men, because all sinned" (Romans 5:12).

Theistic evolution does not acknowledge Adam as the first man, nor that he was created directly from "the dust of the ground" by God (Genesis 2:7). Most theistic evolutionists regard the creation account as being merely a mythical tale, albeit with some spiritual significance. However, the sinner Adam and the Savior Jesus are linked together in the Bible—Romans 5:16–18. Thus, any theological view which mythologizes Adam undermines the biblical basis of Jesus's work of redemption.

Danger no. 7: Loss of biblical chronology

The Bible provides us with a time scale for history and this underlies a proper understanding of the Bible. This time scale includes:

- There is a well-defined beginning in Genesis 1:1, as well as a moment when physical time will end (Matthew 24:14). The time scale cannot be extended indefinitely into the past, nor into the future.

- The total duration of creation was six days (Exodus 20:11).

- The age of the universe may be estimated in terms of the genealogies recorded in the Bible (but note that it cannot be calculated exactly). It is of the order of several thousand years, not billions.

- Galatians 4:4 points out the most outstanding event in the world's history: "But when the fullness of the time had come, God sent forth His Son." This happened nearly 2,000 years ago.

- The return of Christ in power and glory is the greatest expected future event.

Supporters of theistic evolution (and progressive creation) disregard the biblically given measures of time in favor of evolutionist time-scales involving billions of years both past and future (for which there are no convincing physical grounds). This can lead to two errors:

1. Not all statements of the Bible are to be taken seriously.

2. Vigilance concerning the second coming of Jesus may be lost.

Danger no. 8: Loss of creation concepts

Certain essential creation concepts are taught in the Bible. These include:

- God created matter without using any available material.

- God created the earth first, and on the fourth day He added the moon, the solar system, our local galaxy, and all other star systems. This sequence conflicts with all ideas of 'cosmic evolution', such as the "big bang" cosmology.

Theistic evolution ignores all such biblical creation principles and replaces them with evolutionary notions, thereby contradicting and opposing God's omnipotent acts of creation.

Danger no. 9: Misrepresentation of reality

The Bible carries the seal of truth, and all its pronouncements are authoritative—whether they deal with questions of faith and salvation, daily living, or matters of scientific importance.

Evolutionists brush all this aside, e.g. Richard Dawkins says, "Nearly all peoples have developed their own creation myth, and the Genesis story is just the one that happened to have been adopted by one particular tribe of Middle Eastern herders. It has no more special status than the belief of a particular West African tribe that the world was created from the excrement of ants."[4]

If evolution is false, then numerous sciences have embraced false testimony. Whenever these sciences conform to evolutionary views, they misrepresent reality. How much more then a theology which departs from what the Bible says and embraces evolution!

Danger no. 10: Missing the purpose

In no other historical book do we find so many and such valuable statements of purpose for man, as in the Bible. For example:

1. Man is God's purpose in creation (Genesis 1:27–28).

2. Man is the purpose of God's plan of redemption (Isaiah 53:5).

3. Man is the purpose of the mission of God's Son (1 John 4:9).

4. We are the purpose of God's inheritance (Titus 3:7).

5. Heaven is our destination (1 Peter 1:4).

However, the very thought of purposefulness is anathema to evolutionists. "Evolutionary adaptations never follow a purposeful program, they thus cannot be regarded as teleonomical."[5] Thus a belief system such as theistic evolution that marries purposefulness with non-purposefulness is a contradiction in terms.

Conclusion

The doctrines of creation and evolution are so strongly divergent that reconciliation is totally impossible. Theistic evolutionists attempt to integrate the two doctrines, however such syncretism reduces the message of the Bible to insignificance. The conclusion is inevitable: There is no support for theistic evolution in the Bible.

1. This article has been adapted from chapter 8 "The Consequences of Theistic Evolution," from Prof. Dr Werner Gitt's book, *Did God use Evolution?* Christliche Literatur-Verbreitung e.V., Postfach 11 01 35 . 33661, Bielefeld, Germany.

2. E. Jantsch, *Die Selbstorganisation des Universums* (München, 1979), p. 412.

3. Hoimar von Ditfurth, *Wir sind nicht nur von dieser Welt* (München, 1984), pp. 21–22.

4. Richard Dawkins, *The Blind Watchmaker* (Penguin Books, 1986), p. 316.

5. H. Penzlin, *Das Teleologie-Problem in der Biologie*, Biologische Rundschau, 25 (1987), S.7–26, p. 19.

Dr. Werner Gitt has a doctorate in engineering *summa cum laude* from the University of Technology in Aachen, Germany. He is now retired as the director and professor, and Head of the Department of Information Technology, at the German Federal Institute of Physics and Technology.

His written works include *In the Begining was Information, If Animals Could Talk*, and *Did God Use Evolution?*

Could God Really Have Created Everything in Six Days?

by Ken Ham

*I*f the days of creation are really geologic ages of millions of years, then the gospel message is undermined at its foundation because it puts death, disease, thorns, and suffering before the Fall. The effort to define "days" as "geologic ages" results from an erroneous approach to Scripture—reinterpreting the Word of God on the basis of the fallible theories of sinful people.

It is a good exercise to read Genesis 1 and try to put aside outside influences that may cause you to have a predetermined idea of what the word "day" may mean. Just let the words of the passage speak to you.

Taking Genesis 1 in this way, at face value, without doubt it says that God created the universe, the earth, the sun, moon and

stars, plants and animals, and the first two people within six ordinary (approximately 24-hour) days. Being really honest, you would have to admit that you could never get the idea of millions of years from reading this passage.

The majority of Christians (including many Christian leaders) in the Western world, however, do not insist that these days of creation were ordinary-length days, and many of them accept and teach, based on outside influences, that they must have been long periods of time—even millions or billions of years.

How does God communicate to us?

God communicates through language. When He made the first man, Adam, He had already "programmed" him with a language, so there could be communication. Human language consists of words used in a specific context that relates to the entire reality around us.

Thus, God can reveal things to man, and man can communicate with God, because words have meaning and convey an understandable message. If this were not so, how could any of us communicate with each other or with God?

Why "long days"?

Romans 3:4 declares: "Let God be true, and every man a liar."

In *every* instance where someone has *not* accepted the "days" of creation to be ordinary days, they have not allowed the words of Scripture to speak to them in context, as the language requires for communication. They have been influenced by ideas from *outside* of Scripture. Thus, they have set a precedent that could allow any word to be reinterpreted by the preconceived ideas of the person reading the words. Ultimately, this will lead to a communication breakdown, as the same words in the same context could mean different things to different people.

The church fathers

Most church fathers accepted the days of creation as ordinary days.[1] It is true that some of the early church fathers did not teach the days of creation as ordinary days—but many of them had been influenced by Greek philosophy, which caused them to interpret the days as allegorical. They reasoned that the creation days were related to God's activities, and God being timeless meant that the days could not be related to human time.[2] In contrast to today's allegorizers, they could not accept that God took as long as six days.

Thus, the non-literal days resulted from extrabiblical influences (i.e., influences from outside the Bible), not from the words of the Bible.

This approach has affected the way people interpret Scripture to this day. As the man who started the Reformation said,

> The days of creation were ordinary days in length. We must understand that these days were actual days (*veros dies*), contrary to the opinion of the Holy Fathers. Whenever we observe that the opinions of the Fathers disagree with Scripture, we reverently bear with them and acknowledge them to be our elders. Nevertheless, we do not depart from the authority of Scripture for their sake.[3]

Again and again, such leaders admit that Genesis 1, taken in a straightforward way, seems to teach six ordinary days. But they then say that this cannot be because of the age of the universe or some other extrabiblical reason.

Consider the following representative quotes from Bible scholars who are considered to be conservative yet who do not accept the days of creation as ordinary-length days:

> From a superficial reading of Genesis 1, the impression would seem to be that the entire creative process took place in six twenty-four-hour days. . . . This seems to run

counter to modern scientific research, which indicates that the planet Earth was created several billion years ago.[4]

We have shown the possibility of God's having formed the Earth and its life in a series of creative days representing long periods. In view of the apparent age of the Earth, this is not only possible—it is probable.[5]

It is as if these theologians view "nature" as a "67th book of the Bible," albeit with more authority than the 66 written books. Rather, we should consider the words of Charles Haddon Spurgeon, the renowned "prince of preachers," in 1877:

> We are invited, brethren, most earnestly to go away from the old-fashioned belief of our forefathers because of the supposed discoveries of science. What is science? The method by which man tries to conceal his ignorance. It should not be so, but so it is. You are not to be dogmatical in theology, my brethren, it is wicked; but for scientific men it is the correct thing. You are never to assert anything very strongly; but scientists may boldly assert what they cannot prove, and may demand a faith far more credulous than any we possess. Forsooth, you and I are to take our Bibles and shape and mould our belief according to the evershifting teachings of so-called scientific men. What folly is this! Why, the march of science, falsely so called, through the world may be traced by exploded fallacies and abandoned theories. Former explorers once adored are now ridiculed; the continual wreckings of false hypotheses is a matter of universal notoriety. You may tell where the learned have encamped by the debris left behind of suppositions and theories as plentiful as broken bottles.[6]

Those who would use historical science (as propounded by people who, by and large, ignore God's written revelation) to interpret the Bible, to teach us things about God, have matters front to back. Because we are fallen, fallible creatures, we need God's written Word, illuminated by the Holy Spirit, to properly understand natural history. The respected systematic theologian Berkhof said:

> Since the entrance of sin into the world, man can gather true knowledge about God from His general revelation only if he studies it in the light of Scripture, in which the elements of God's original self-revelation, which were obscured and perverted by the blight of sin, are republished, corrected, and interpreted. . . . Some are inclined to speak of God's general revelation as a second source; but this is hardly correct in view of the fact that nature can come into consideration here only as interpreted in the light of Scripture.[7]

In other words, Christians should build their thinking on the Bible, not on science.

The "days" of Genesis 1

What does the Bible tell us about the meaning of "day" in Genesis 1? A word can have more than one meaning, depending on the context. For instance, the English word "day" can have perhaps 14 different meanings. For example, consider the following sentence: "Back in my grandfather's day, it took 12 days to drive across the country during the day."

Here the first occurrence of "day" means "time" in a general sense. The second "day," where a number is used, refers to an ordinary day, and the third refers to the daylight portion of the 24-hour period. The point is that words can have more than one meaning, depending on the context.

To understand the meaning of "day" in Genesis 1, we need to determine how the Hebrew word for "day," *yom*, is used in the context of Scripture. Consider the following:

- A typical concordance will illustrate that *yom* can have a range of meanings: a period of light as contrasted to night, a 24-hour period, time, a specific point of time, or a year.

- A classic, well-respected Hebrew-English lexicon[8] (a dictionary) has seven headings and many subheadings for the meaning of *yom*—but it defines the creation days of Genesis 1 as ordinary days under the heading "day as defined by evening and morning."

- A number and the phrase "evening and morning" are used with each of the six days of creation (Gen. 1:5, 8, 13, 19, 23, 31).

- Outside Genesis 1, *yom* is used with a number 359 times, and each time it means an ordinary day.[9] Why would Genesis 1 be the exception?[10]

- Outside Genesis 1, *yom* is used with the word "evening" or "morning"[11] 23 times. "Evening" and "morning" appear in association, but without *yom*, 38 times. All 61 times the text refers to an ordinary day. Why would Genesis 1 be the exception?[12]

- In Genesis 1:5, *yom* occurs in context with the word "night." Outside of Genesis 1, "night" is used with *yom* 53 times, and each time it means an ordinary day. Why would Genesis 1 be the exception? Even the usage of the word "light" with *yom* in this passage determines the meaning as ordinary day.[13]

- The plural of *yom*, which does not appear in Genesis 1, can be used to communicate a longer time period, such as "in those days."[14] Adding a number here would be nonsensical. Clearly, in Exodus 20:11, where a number is used with "days," it unambiguously refers to six earth-rotation days.

- There are words in biblical Hebrew (such as olam or qedem) that are very suitable for communicating long periods of time, or indefinite time, but none of these words are used in

Genesis 1.[15] Alternatively, the days or years could have been compared with grains of sand if long periods were meant.

Dr. James Barr (Regius Professor of Hebrew at Oxford University), who himself does not believe Genesis is true history, nonetheless admitted as far as the language of Genesis 1 is concerned that

> So far as I know, there is no professor of Hebrew or Old Testament at any world-class university who does not believe that the writer(s) of Gen. 1–11 intended to convey to their readers the ideas that (a) creation took place in a series of six days which were the same as the days of 24 hours we now experience (b) the figures contained in the Genesis genealogies provided by simple addition a chronology from the beginning of the world up to later stages in the biblical story (c) Noah's Flood was understood to be worldwide and extinguish all human and animal life except for those in the ark.[16]

In like manner, nineteenth century liberal Professor Marcus Dods, New College, Edinburgh, said,

> If, for example, the word "day" in these chapters does not mean a period of twenty-four hours, the interpretation of Scripture is hopeless.[17]

Conclusion about "day" in Genesis 1

If we are prepared to let the words of the language speak to us in accord with the context and normal definitions, without being influenced by outside ideas, then the word for "day" found in Genesis 1—which is qualified by a number, the phrase "evening and morning" and for Day 1 the words "light and darkness"—obviously means an ordinary day (about 24 hours).

In Martin Luther's day, some of the church fathers were saying that God created everything in only one day or in an instant.

Martin Luther wrote:

> When Moses writes that God created Heaven and Earth and whatever is in them in six days, then let this period continue to have been six days, and do not venture to devise any comment according to which six days were one day. But, if you cannot understand how this could have been done in six days, then grant the Holy Spirit the honor of being more learned than you are. For you are to deal with Scripture in such a way that you bear in mind that God Himself says what is written. But since God is speaking, it is not fitting for you wantonly to turn His Word in the direction you wish to go.[18]

Similarly, John Calvin stated, "Albeit the duration of the world, now declining to its ultimate end, has not yet attained six thousand years. . . . God's work was completed not in a moment but in six days."[19]

Luther and Calvin were the backbone of the Protestant Reformation that called the church back to Scripture—Sola Scriptura (Scripture alone). Both of these men were adamant that Genesis 1 taught six ordinary days of creation—only thousands of years ago.

Why six days?

Exodus 31:12 says that God commanded Moses to say to the children of Israel:

> Six days may work be done, but on the seventh is the sabbath of rest, holy to the Lord. Whoever does any work in the Sabbath day, he shall surely be put to death. Therefore the sons of Israel shall keep the Sabbath, to observe the Sabbath throughout their generations, for an everlasting covenant. It is a sign between me and the sons of Israel forever. For in six days the Lord made the heavens and

the earth, and on the seventh day He rested, and was refreshed (Exodus 31:15–17).

Then God gave Moses two tablets of stone upon which were written the commandments of God, written by the finger of God (Exodus 31:18).

Because God is infinite in power and wisdom, there's no doubt He could have created the universe and its contents in no time at all, or six seconds, or six minutes, or six hours—after all, with God nothing shall be impossible (Luke 1:37).

However, the question to ask is, "Why did God take so long? Why as long as six days?" The answer is also given in Exodus 20:11, and that answer is the basis of the Fourth Commandment:

For in six days the LORD made the heavens and the earth, the sea, and all that is in them, and rested the seventh

day. Therefore the LORD blessed the Sabbath day and hallowed it.

The seven-day week has no basis outside of Scripture. In this Old Testament passage, God commands His people, Israel, to work for six days and rest for one—thus giving us a reason why He deliberately took as long as six days to create everything. He set the example for man. Our week is patterned after this principle. Now if He created everything in six thousand (or six million) years, followed by a rest of one thousand or one million years, then we would have a very interesting week indeed.

Some say that Exodus 20:11 is only an analogy in the sense that man is to work and rest—not that it was to mean six literal ordinary days followed by one literal ordinary day. However, Bible scholars have shown that this commandment "does not use analogy or archetypal thinking but that its emphasis is 'stated in terms of the imitation of God or a divine precedent that is to be followed.'"[20] In other words, it was to be six literal days of work, followed by one literal day of rest, just as God worked for six literal days and rested for one.

Some have argued that "the heavens and the earth" is just earth and perhaps the solar system, not the whole universe. However, this verse clearly says that God made everything in six days—six consecutive ordinary days, just like the commandment in the previous verse to work for six consecutive ordinary days.

The phrase "heaven(s) and earth" in Scripture is an example of a figure of speech called a merism, where two opposites are combined into an all-encompassing single concept, in this case the totality of creation. A linguistic analysis of the words "heaven(s) and earth" in Scripture shows that they refer to the totality of all creation (the Hebrews did not have a word for "universe"). For example, in Genesis 14:19 God is called "Creator of heaven and earth." In Jeremiah 23:24 God speaks of Himself as filling "heaven and earth." See also Genesis 14:22; 2 Kings 19:15; 2 Chronicles 2:12; Psalms 115: 15, 121:2, 124:8, 134:3, 146:6; and Isaiah 37:16.

Thus, there is no scriptural warrant for restricting Exodus 20:11 to earth and its atmosphere or the solar system alone. So Exodus 20:11 does show that the whole universe was created in six ordinary days.

Implication

As the days of creation are ordinary days in length, then by adding up the years in Scripture (assuming no gaps in the genealogies[21]), the age of the universe is only about six thousand years.[22]

Refuting common objections to six literal days

Objection 1

"Science" has shown the earth and universe are billions of years old; therefore the "days" of creation must be long periods (or indefinite periods) of time.

Answer

1. The age of the earth, as determined by man's fallible methods, is based on unproven assumptions, so it is not proven that the earth is billions of years old.[23]

2. This unproven age is being used to force an interpretation on the language of the Bible. Thus, man's fallible theories are allowed to interpret the Bible. This ultimately undermines the use of language to communicate.

3. Evolutionary scientists claim the fossil layers over the earth's surface date back hundreds of millions of years. As soon as one allows millions of years for the fossil layers, then one has accepted death, bloodshed, disease, thorns, and suffering before Adam's sin.

The Bible makes it clear[24] that death, bloodshed, disease, thorns, and suffering are a consequence of sin.[25] In Genesis 1:29–30, God gave Adam and Eve and the animals plants to eat (this is reading Genesis at face value, as literal history, as Jesus did in Matthew 19:3–6). In fact, there is a theological distinction made between animals and plants. Human beings and higher animals are described in Genesis 1 as having a *nephesh*, or life principle. (This is true of at least the vertebrate land animals as well as the birds and fish: Genesis 1:20, 24.) Plants do not have this *nephesh*—they are not "alive" in the same sense animals are. They were given for food.

Man was permitted to eat meat only after the Flood (Genesis 9:3). This makes it obvious that the statements in Genesis 1:29–30 were meant to inform us that man and the animals were vegetarian to start with. Also, in Genesis 9:2, we are told of a change God apparently made in the way animals react to man.

God warned Adam in Genesis 2:17 that if he ate of the "tree of the knowledge of good and evil" he would "die." The Hebrew grammar actually means, "dying, you will die." In other words, it would be the commencement of a process of physical dying (see Genesis 3:19). It also clearly involved spiritual death (separation from God).

After Adam disobeyed God, the Lord clothed Adam and Eve with "coats of skins" (Genesis 3:21).[26] To do this He must have killed and shed the blood of at least one animal. The reason for this can be summed up by Hebrews 9:22:

And according to the law almost all things are purified with blood, and without shedding of blood there is no remission.

God requires the shedding of blood for the remission of sins. What happened in the garden was a picture of what was to come in Jesus Christ, who shed His blood on the Cross as the Lamb of God who took away the sin of the world (John 1:29).

Now if the Garden of Eden were sitting on a fossil record of dead things millions of years old, then blood was shed before sin.

This would destroy the foundation of the Atonement. The Bible is clear: the sin of Adam brought death and suffering into the world. As Romans 8:19–22 tells us, the whole of creation "groans" because of the effects of the fall of Adam, and the creation will be liberated "from the bondage of corruption into the glorious liberty of the children of God" (Rom. 8:21). Also, bear in mind that thorns came into existence after the Curse. Because there are thorns in the fossil record, it had to be formed after Adam and Eve sinned.

The pronouncement of the death penalty on Adam was both a curse and a blessing. A curse because death is horrible and continually reminds us of the ugliness of sin; a blessing because it meant the consequences of sin—separation from fellowship with God—need not be eternal. Death stopped Adam and his descendants from living in a state of sin, with all its consequences, forever. And because death was the just penalty for sin, Jesus Christ suffered physical death, shedding His blood, to release Adam's descendants from the consequences of sin. The Apostle Paul discusses this in depth in Romans 5 and 1 Corinthians 15.

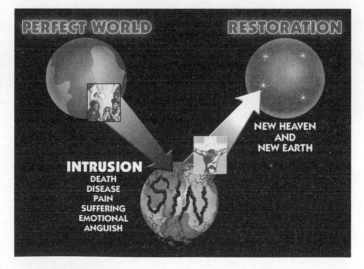

Revelation 21–22 makes it clear that there will be a "new heavens and a new earth" one day, where there will be "no more death" and "no more curse"—just like it was before sin changed everything. If there are to be animals as part of the new earth, obviously they will not be dying or eating each other, nor eating the redeemed people!

Thus, adding the supposed millions of years to Scripture destroys the foundations of the message of the Cross.

Objection 2

According to Genesis 1, the sun was not created until Day 4. How could there be day and night (ordinary days) without the sun for the first three days?

Answer

1. Again, it is important for us to let the language of God's Word speak to us. If we come to Genesis 1 without any outside influences, as has been shown, each of the six days of creation appears with the Hebrew word *yom* qualified by a number and the phrase "evening and morning." The first three days are written the same way as the next three. So if we let the language speak to us, all six days were ordinary earth days.

2. The sun is not needed for day and night. What is needed is light and a rotating earth. On the first day of creation, God made light (Genesis 1:3). The phrase "evening and morning" certainly implies a rotating earth. Thus, if we have light from one direction, and a spinning earth, there can be day and night.

Where did the light come from? We are not told,[27] but Genesis 1:3 certainly indicates it was a created light to provide day and night until God made the sun on Day 4 to rule the day. Revelation 21:23 tells us that one day the sun will not be needed because the glory of God will light the heavenly city.

Perhaps one reason God did it this way was to illustrate that the sun did not have the priority in the creation that people have tended to give it. The sun did not give birth to the earth as evolutionary theories postulate; the sun was God's created tool to rule the day that God had made (Genesis 1:16).

Down through the ages, people such as the Egyptians have worshiped the sun. God warned the Israelites, in Deuteronomy 4:19, not to worship the sun as the pagan cultures around them did. They were commanded to worship the God who made the sun—not the sun that was *made* by God.

Evolutionary theories (the "big bang" hypothesis for instance) state that the sun came before the earth and that the sun's energy on the earth eventually gave rise to life. Just as in pagan beliefs, the sun is, in a sense, given credit for the wonder of creation.

It is interesting to contrast the speculations of modern cosmology with the writings of the early church father Theophilus:

> On the fourth day the luminaries came into existence. Since God has foreknowledge, he understood the nonsense of the foolish philosophers who were going to say that the things produced on Earth came from the stars, so that they might set God aside. In order therefore that the truth might be demonstrated, plants and seeds came into existence before stars. For what comes into existence later cannot cause what is prior to it.[28]

Objection 3

2 Peter 3:8 *states that "one day is with the Lord as a thousand years," therefore the days of creation could be long periods of time.*

Answer

1. This passage has no creation context—it is not referring to Genesis or the six days of creation.

2. This verse has what is called a "comparative article"—"as" or "like"—which is not found in Genesis 1. In other words, it is not saying a day is a thousand years; it is comparing a real, literal day to a real, literal thousand years. The context of this passage is the Second Coming of Christ. It is saying that, to God, a day is like a thousand years, because God is outside of time. God is not limited by natural processes and time as humans are. What may seem like a long time to us (e.g., waiting for the Second Coming), or a short time, is nothing to God, either way.

3. The second part of the verse reads "and a thousand years as one day," which, in essence, cancels out the first part of the verse for those who want to equate a day with a thousand years. Thus, it cannot be saying a day is a thousand years or vice versa.

4. Psalm 90:4 states, "For a thousand years in your sight are as yesterday when it is past, and as a watch in the night." Here a thousand years is being compared with a "watch in the night" (four hours[29]). Because the phrase "watch in the night" is joined in a particular way to "yesterday," it is saying that a thousand years is being compared with a short period of time—not simply to a day.

5. If one used this passage to claim that "day" in the Bible means a thousand years, then, to be consistent, one would have to say that Jonah was in the belly of the fish three thousand years, or that Jesus has not yet risen from the dead after two thousand years in the grave.

Objection 4

Insisting on six solar days for creation limits God, whereas allowing God billions of years does not limit Him.

Answer

Actually, insisting on six ordinary earth-rotation days of creation is not limiting *God*, but limiting *us* to believing that God actually did what He tells us in His Word. Also, if God created everything in six days, as the Bible says, then surely this reveals the power and wisdom of God in a profound way— Almighty God did not *need* eons of time. However, the billions-of-years scenarios diminish God by suggesting that mere chance could create things or that God needed huge amounts of time to create things—this would be limiting God's power by reducing it to naturalistic explanations.

Objection 5

Adam could not have accomplished all that the Bible states in one day (Day 6). He could not have named all the animals, for instance; there was not enough time.

Answer

Adam did not have to name *all* the animals—only those God brought to him. For instance, Adam was commanded to name "every beast of the field" (Genesis 2:20), not "beast of the earth"

(Genesis 1:25). The phrase "beast of the field" is most likely a subset of the larger group "beast of the earth." He did not have to name "everything that creeps upon the earth" (Genesis 1:25) or any of the sea creatures. Also, the number of "kinds" would be much less than the number of species in today's classification.

When critics say that Adam could not name the animals in less than one day, what they really mean is they do not understand how *they* could do it, so Adam could not. However, our brain has suffered from 6,000 years of the Curse—it has been greatly affected by the Fall. Before sin, Adam's brain was perfect.

When God made Adam, He must have programmed him with a perfect language. Today we program computers to "speak" and "remember." How much more could our Creator God have created Adam as a mature human (he was not born as a baby needing to learn to speak), having in his memory a perfect language with a perfect understanding of each word. (That is why Adam understood what God meant when he said he would "die" if he disobeyed, even though he had not seen any death.) Adam may also have had a "perfect" memory (something like a photographic memory, perhaps).

It would have been no problem for this first perfect man to make up words and name the animals God brought to him and remember the names—in far less than one day.[30]

Objection 6

Genesis 2 *is a different account of creation, with a different order, so how can the first chapter be accepted as teaching six literal days?*

Answer

Actually, Genesis 2 is not a different account of creation. It is a more detailed account of Day 6 of creation. Chapter 1 is an overview of the whole of creation; chapter 2 gives details surrounding the creation of the garden, the first man, and his activities on Day 6.[31]

Between the creation of Adam and the creation of Eve, the King James Version says, "Out of the ground the Lord God formed every beast of the field and every fowl of the air" (Genesis 2:19). This seems to say that the land beasts and birds were created between the creation of Adam and Eve. However, Jewish scholars did not recognize any such conflict with the account in chapter 1, where Adam and Eve were both created after the beasts and birds (Genesis 1:23–25). There is no contradiction, because in Hebrew the precise tense of a verb is determined by the context. It is clear from chapter 1 that the beasts and birds were created before Adam, so Jewish scholars would have understood the verb "formed" to mean "had formed" or "having formed" in Genesis 2:19 If we translate verse 19, "Now the Lord God had formed out of the ground all the beasts of the field," the apparent disagreement with Genesis 1 disappears completely.

Regarding the plants and herbs in Genesis 2:5 and the trees in Genesis 2:9 (compare with Genesis 1:12), the plants and herbs are described as "of the field" and they needed a man to tend them. These are clearly cultivated plants, not just plants in general (Genesis 1). Also, the trees (Genesis 2:9) are only the trees planted in the garden, not trees in general.

In Matthew 19:3–6 Jesus Christ quotes from both Genesis 1:27 and Genesis 2:24 when referring to the *same man and woman* in teaching the doctrine of marriage. Clearly, Jesus saw them as *complementary* accounts, *not* contradictory ones.

Objection 7

There is no "evening and morning" for the seventh day of the Creation Week (Genesis 2:2). Thus, we must still be in the "seventh day," so none of the days can be ordinary days.

Answer

Look again at the section entitled "Why Six Days?" above. Exodus 20:11 is clearly referring to seven literal days—six for work and one for rest.

Also, God stated that He "rested" from His work of creation (not that He is resting!). The fact that He rested from His work of creation does not preclude Him from continuing to rest from this activity. God's work now is different—it is a work of sustaining His creation and of reconciliation and redemption because of man's sin.

The word *yom* is qualified by a number (Genesis 2:2–3), so the context still determines that it is an ordinary solar day. Also, God blessed this seventh day and made it holy. In Genesis 3:17–19 we read of the Curse on the earth because of sin. Paul refers to this in Romans 8:22. It does not make sense that God would call this day holy and blessed if He cursed the ground on this "day." We live in a sin-cursed earth—we are not in the seventh blessed holy day!

Note that in arguing that the seventh day is not an ordinary day because it is not associated with "evening and morning," proponents are tacitly agreeing that the other six days are ordinary days because they are defined by an evening and a morning.

Some have argued that Hebrews 4:3–4 implies that the seventh day is continuing today:

For we who have believed do enter that rest, as He has said: "So I swore in My wrath, 'They shall not enter My rest,'" although the works were finished from the foundation of the world. For He has spoken in a certain place of the seventh day in this way: "And God rested on the seventh day from all His works... ."

However, verse 4 reiterates that God rested (past tense) on the seventh day. If someone says on Monday that he rested on Friday and is still resting, this would not suggest that Friday continued through to Monday! Also, only those who have believed in Christ will enter that rest, showing that it is a spiritual rest, which is compared with God's rest since the Creation Week. It is not some sort of continuation of the seventh day (otherwise everyone would be "in" this rest).[32]

Hebrews does not say that the seventh day of Creation Week is continuing today, merely that the rest He instituted is continuing.

Objection 8

Genesis 2:4 states, "In the day that the Lord God made the earth and the heavens." As this refers to all six days of creation, it shows that the word "day" does not mean an ordinary day.

Answer

The Hebrew word *yom* as used here is *not* qualified by a number, the phrase "evening and morning," or light or darkness. In this context, the verse really means "in the time God created" (referring to the Creation Week) or "when God created."

Other problems with long days and similar interpretations

- If the plants made on Day 3 were separated by millions of years from the birds and nectar bats (created Day 5) and insects (created Day 6) necessary for their pollination, then such plants could not have survived. This problem would be especially acute for species with complex symbiotic relationships (each depending on the other; e.g., the yucca plant and the associated moth[33]).

- Adam was created on Day 6, lived through Day 7, and then died when he was 930 years old (Genesis 5:5). If each day were a thousand years or millions of years, this would make no sense of Adam's age at death.

- Some have claimed that the word for "made" (*asah*) in Exodus 20:11 actually means "show." They propose that God showed or revealed the information about creation to Moses during a six-day period. This allows for the creation itself to have occurred over millions of years. However, "showed" is not a valid translation for *asah*. Its meaning covers "to make, manufacture, produce, do," etc., but not "to show" in the sense of reveal.[34] Where *asah* is translated as "show"—for example, "show kindness" (Genesis 24:12)—it is in the sense of "to do" or "make" kindness.

- Some have claimed that because the word *asah* is used for the creation of the sun, moon, and stars on Day 4, and not the word *bara*, which is used in Genesis 1:1 for "create," this means God only revealed the sun, moon, and stars at this stage. They insist the word *asah* has the meaning of "revealed." In other words, the luminaries were supposedly already in existence and were only revealed at this stage. However, *bara* and *asah* are used in Scripture to describe the same event. For example, *asah* is used in Exodus 20:11 to refer to the creation of the heavens and the earth, but *bara* is used to refer to the creation of the heavens and the earth in Genesis 1:1. The word *asah* is used concerning the creation of the first people in Genesis 1:26—they did not previously exist. And then they are said to have been created (*bara*) in Genesis 1:27. There are many other similar examples. *asah* has a broad range of meanings involving "to do" or "to make," which includes *bara* creation.

- Some accept that the days of creation are ordinary days as far as the language of Genesis is concerned but not as literal days of history as far as man is concerned. This is basically the view called the "framework hypothesis."[35] This is a very complex and contrived view which has been thoroughly refuted by scholars.[36]

The real purpose of the framework hypothesis can be seen in the following quote from an article by one of its proponents:

To rebut the literalist interpretation of the Genesis creation "week" propounded by the young-earth theorists is a central concern of this article.[37]

Some people want the days of creation to be long periods in an attempt to harmonize evolution or billions of years with the Bible's account of origins. However, the order of events according to long-age beliefs does not agree with that of Genesis. Consider the following table:

Contradictions between the order of creation in the Bible and evolution/long-ages

Biblical account of creation	Evolutionary/long-age speculation
Earth before the sun and stars	Stars and sun before earth
Earth covered in water initially	Earth a molten blob initially
Oceans first, then dry land	Dry land, then the oceans
Life first created on the land	Life started in the oceans
Plants created before the sun	Plants came long after the sun
Land animals created after birds	Land animals existed before birds
Whales before land animals	Land animals before whales

Clearly, those who do not accept the six literal days are the ones reading their own preconceived ideas into the passage.

Long-age compromises

Other than the "gap theory" (the belief that there is a gap of indeterminate time between the first two verses of Genesis 1), the major compromise positions that try to harmonize long ages and/or evolution with Genesis fall into two categories:

1. "theistic evolution" wherein God supposedly directed the evolutionary process of millions of years, or even just set it up and let it run, and

2. "progressive creation" where God supposedly intervened in the processes of death and struggle to create millions of species at various times over millions of years.

All long-age compromises reject Noah's Flood as global—it could only be a local event because the fossil layers are accepted as evidence for millions of years. A global Flood would have destroyed this record and produced another. Therefore, these positions cannot allow a catastrophic global Flood that would form layers of fossil-bearing rocks over the earth. This, of course, goes against Scripture, which obviously teaches a global Flood (Genesis 6–9).[38] Sadly, most theologians years ago simply tried to add this belief to the Bible instead of realizing that these layers were laid down by Noah's Flood.

Does it really matter?

Yes, it does matter what a Christian believes concerning the days of creation in Genesis 1. Most importantly, all schemes which insert eons of time into, or before, creation undermine the gospel by putting death, bloodshed, disease, thorns, and suffering before sin and the Fall, as explained above (see answer to Objection 1). Here are two more reasons:

1. It is really a matter of how one approaches the Bible, in principle. If we do not allow the language to speak to us in context, but try to make the text fit ideas outside of Scripture, then ultimately the meaning of any word in any part of the Bible depends on man's interpretation, which can change according to whatever outside ideas are in vogue.

2. If one allows science (which has wrongly become synonymous with evolution and materialism) to determine our

understanding of Scripture, then this can lead to a slippery slope of unbelief through the rest of Scripture. For instance, science would proclaim that a person cannot be raised from the dead. Does this mean we should interpret the Resurrection of Christ to reflect this? Sadly, some do just this, saying that the Resurrection simply means that Jesus' teachings live on in His followers.

When people accept at face value what Genesis is teaching and accept the days as ordinary days, they will have no problem accepting and making sense of the rest of the Bible.

Martin Luther once said:

> I have often said that whoever would study Holy Scripture should be sure to see to it that he stays with the simple words as long as he can and by no means departs from them unless an article of faith compels him to understand them differently. For of this we must be certain: no clearer speech has been heard on Earth than what God has spoken.[39]

Pure words

God's people need to realize that the Word of God is something very special. It is not just the words of men. As Paul said in 1 Thessalonians 2:13, "You received it not as the word of men, but as it is, truly the word of God."

Proverbs 30:5–6 states that "every word of God is pure ... . Do not add to His words, lest He reprove you and you be found a liar." The Bible cannot be treated as just some great literary work. We need to "tremble at his word" (Isaiah 6:5) and not forget:

> All Scripture is given by inspiration of God, and is profitable for doctrine, for reproof, for correction, for instruction in righteousness, that the man of God may be complete, thoroughly equipped for every good work (2 Timothy 3:16–17).

In the original autographs, every word and letter in the Bible is there because God put it there. Let us listen to God speaking to us through His Word and not arrogantly think we can tell God what He really means!

1. M. Van Bebber and P. Taylor, *Creation and Time: A Report on the Progressive Creationist Book by Hugh Ross* (Films for Christ, 1994).

2. G. Hasel, "The 'days' of creation in Genesis 1: literal 'days' or figurative 'periods/epochs' of time? *Origins* 21(1):5–38, 1994.

3. Martin Luther as cited in E. Plass, *What Martin Luther Says: A Practical In-Home Anthology for the Active Christian* (Concordia Publishing House, 1991), p. 1523.

4. G. Archer, *A Survey of Old Testament Introduction* (Moody Press, 1994), pp. 196–197.

5. J. Boice, *Genesis: An Expositional Commentary*, Vol. 1, *Genesis 1:1–11* (Zondervan Publishing House, 1982), p. 68.

6. C.H. Spurgeon, *The Sword and the Trowel*, 1877, p. 197.

7. L. Berkhof, Introductory volume to *Systematic Theology* (Wm. B. Eerdmans, 1946), pp. 60, 96.

8. F. Brown, S. Driver, and C. Briggs, *A Hebrew and English Lexicon of the Old Testament* (Clarendon Press, 1951), p. 398.

9. Some say that Hosea 6:2 is an exception to this because of the figurative language. However, the Hebrew idiomatic expression used, "After two days ... in the third day," meaning "in a short time," makes sense only if "day" is understood in its normal sense.

10. J. Stambaugh, "The days of creation: a semantic approach," *TJ* 5(1):70–78, April 1991. Available online at www.answersingenesis.org/go/days.

11. The Jews start their day in the evening (sundown followed by night), obviously based on the fact that Genesis begins the day with the "evening."

12. Stambaugh, "The days of creation: a semantic approach," p. 75.

13. Ibid., p. 72.

14. Ibid., pp. 72–73.

15. Stambaugh, "The days of creation: a semantic approach," pp. 73–74; R. Grigg, "How long were the days of Genesis 1?" *Creation* 19(1):23–25, 1996.

16. J. Barr, personal letter to David Watson, April 23, 1984.

17. M. Dods, *Expositor's Bible* (T & T Clark, 1888), p. 4, as cited by D. Kelly, *Creation and Change* (Christian Focus Publications, 1997), p. 112.

18. Plass, *What Martin Luther Says: A Practical In-Home Anthology for the Active Christian*, p. 1523.

19. J. McNeil, Ed., *Calvin: Institutes of the Christian Religion 1* (Westminster Press, 1960), pp. 160–161, 182.

20. G. Hasel, "The 'days' of creation in Genesis 1: literal 'days' or figurative 'periods/epochs' of time? p. 29.

21. J. Whitcomb and H. Morris, *The Genesis Flood* (Presbyterian and Reformed Publ., 1961), pp. 481–483, Appendix II. They allow for the possibility of gaps in the genealogies because the word "begat" can skip generations. However, they point out that even allowing for gaps would give a maximum age of around 10,000 years.

22. L. Pierce, "The forgotten archbishop," *Creation* 20(2):42–43, 1998. Ussher carried out a very scholarly work in adding up all the years in Scripture to obtain a date of creation of 4004 BC. Ussher has been mocked for stating that creation occurred on October 23—he obtained this date by working backward using the Jewish civil year and accounting for how the year and month were derived over the years. Thus, he didn't just pull this date out of the air but gave a scholarly mathematical basis for it. This is not to say this is the correct date, as there are assumptions involved, but the point is, his work is not to be scoffed at. Ussher did *not* specify the hour of the day for creation, as some skeptics assert. Young's *Analytical Concordance*, under "creation," lists many other authorities, including extrabiblical ones, who all give a date for creation of less than 10,000 years ago.

23. See the two chapters on radiometric dating by Mike Riddle in *The New Answers Book 1* (Master Books, 2006) on these dating methods to see the assumptions involved. See also H. Morris and J. Morris, *Science, Scripture, and the Young Earth* (Institute for Creation Research, 1989), pp. 39–44; J. Morris, *The Young Earth* (Master Books, 1996), pp. 51–67; S. Austin, *Grand Canyon: Monument to Catastrophe* (Institute for Creation Research, 1994), pp. 111–131; L. Vardiman, ed., *Radio Isotopes and the Age of the Earth, Vol. 2* (Master Books, 2005).

24. K. Ham, *The Lie: Evolution* (Master Books, 1987), Introduction, pp. xiii–xiv; K. Ham, "The necessity for believing in six literal days," *Creation* 18(1):38–41, 1996; K. Ham, "The wrong way round!" *Creation* 18(3):38–41, 1996; K. Ham, "Fathers, promises and vegemite," *Creation* 19(1):14–17, 1997; K. Ham, "The narrow road," *Creation* 19(2):47–49, 1997; K. Ham, "Millions of years and the 'doctrine of Balaam,'" *Creation* 19(3):15–17, 1997.

25. J. Gill, *A Body of Doctrinal and Practical Divinity*, 1760. Republished by Primitive Baptist Library, 1980, p. 191. This is not just a new idea from modern scholars. In 1760 John Gill, in his commentaries, insisted there was no death, bloodshed, disease, or suffering before sin.

26. All Eve's progeny, except the God-man Jesus Christ, were born with original sin (Romans 5:12,18–19), so Eve could not have conceived when she was sinless. So the Fall must have occurred fairly quickly, before Eve had conceived any children (they were told to be "fruitful and multiply").

27. Some people ask why God did not tell us the source of this light. However, if God told us everything, we would have so many books we would not have time to read them. God has given us all the information we need to come to the right conclusions about the things that really matter.

28. L. Lavallee, "The early church defended creation science," *Impact*, No. 160, p. ii, 1986. Quotation from *Theophilus "To Autolycus,"* 2.8, Oxford Early Christian Texts.

29. The Jews had three watches during the night (sunset to 10 pm; 10 pm to 2 am; 2 am to sunrise), but the Romans had four watches, beginning at 6 pm.

30. R. Grigg, "Naming the animals: all in a day's work for Adam," *Creation* 18(4):46–49, 1996.

31. D. Batten, "Genesis contradictions?" *Creation* 18(4):44–45, 1996; M. Kruger, "An understanding of Genesis 2:5," *CEN Technical Journal* 11(1):106–110, 1997.

32. Anon., "Is the Seventh Day an eternal day?" *Creation* 21(3):44–45, 1999.

33. F. Meldau, *Why We Believe in Creation Not in Evolution* (Christian Victory Publ., 1972), pp. 114–116.

34. Nothing in Gesenius's *Lexicon* supports the interpretation of *asah* as "show"; See Charles Taylor's "Days of Revelation or creation?" (1997) found at www.answersingenesis.org/docs/188.asp.

35. M. Kline, "Because it had not rained," *Westminster Theological Journal* 20:146–157, 1957–1958.

36. Kruger, "An understanding of Genesis 2:5," pp. 106–110; J. Pipa, "From chaos to cosmos: a critique of the framework hypothesis," presented at the Far-Western Regional Annual Meeting of the Evangelical Theological Society, USA, April 26, 1996; Wayne Grudem's *Systematic Theology* (InterVarsity Press, 1994), pp. 302–305, summarizes the framework hypothesis and its problems and inconsistencies.

37. M. Kline, "Space and time in the Genesis cosmology," *Perspectives on Science & Christian Faith* 48(1), 1996.

38. M. Van Bebber and P. Taylor, *Creation and Time: A Report on the Progressive Creationist Book by Hugh Ross*, pp. 55–59; Whitcomb and Morris, *The Genesis Flood*, pp. 212–330.

39. Plass, *What Martin Luther Says: A Practical In-Home Anthology for the Active Christian*, p. 93.

Why Shouldn't Christians Accept Millions of Years?

by Terry Mortenson

There is an intensifying controversy in the church all over the world regarding the age of the earth. For the first 18 centuries of church history, the almost universal belief of Christians was that God created the world in six literal days roughly 4,000 years before Christ and destroyed the world with a global Flood at the time of Noah.

But about 200 years ago some scientists developed new theories of earth history, which proposed that the earth and universe are millions of years old. Over the past 200 years Christian leaders have made various attempts to fit the millions of years into the Bible. These include the day-age view, gap theory, local flood view, framework hypothesis, theistic evolution, and progressive creation.

A growing number of Christians (now called young-earth creationists), including many scientists, hold to the traditional view, believing it to be the only view that is truly faithful to Scripture and that fits the scientific evidence far better than the reigning old-earth evolutionary theory.

Many Christians say that the age of the earth is an unimportant and divisive side issue that hinders the proclamation of the gospel. But is that really the case? Answers in Genesis and many other creationist organizations think not.

In this chapter, I want to introduce you to some of the reasons we think that Christians cannot accept the millions of years without doing great damage to the church and her witness in the world. Other chapters in this book will go into much more detail on these issues.

1. **The Bible clearly teaches that God created in six literal, 24-hour days a few thousand years ago.** The Hebrew word for day in Genesis 1 is *yom*. In the vast majority of its uses in the Old Testament it means a literal day; and where it doesn't, the context makes this clear.

2. **The context of Genesis 1 clearly shows that the days of creation were literal days.** First, *yom* is defined the first time it is used in the Bible (Genesis 1:4–5) in its two literal senses: the light portion of the light/dark cycle and the whole light/dark cycle. Second, *yom* is used with "evening" and "morning." Everywhere these two words are used in the Old Testament, either together or separately and with or without *yom* in the context, they always mean a literal evening or morning of a literal day. Third, *yom* is modified with a number: one day, second day, third day, etc., which everywhere else in the Old

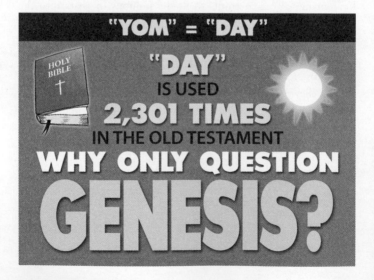

Testament indicates literal days. Fourth, *yom* is defined literally in Genesis 1:14 in relation to the heavenly bodies.

3. **The genealogies of Genesis 5 and 11 make it clear that the creation days happened only about 6,000 years ago.** It is transparent from the genealogies of Genesis 5 and 11 (which give very detailed chronological information, unlike the clearly abbreviated genealogy in Matthew 1 and other chronological information in the Bible that the Creation Week took place only about 6,000 years ago.

4. **Exodus 20:9–11 blocks all attempts to fit millions of years into Genesis 1.** "Six days you shall labor and do all your work, but the seventh day is a sabbath of the LORD your God; in it you shall not do any work, you or your son or your daughter, your male or your female servant or your cattle or your sojourner who stays with you. For in six days the LORD made the heavens and the earth, the sea and all that is in them, and rested on the seventh day; therefore the LORD blessed the sabbath day and made it holy" (Exodus 20:9-11).

This passage gives the reason for God's command to Israel to work six days and then take a sabbath rest. *Yom* is used in both parts of the commandment. If God meant that the Jews were to work six days because He created over six long periods of time, He could have said that using one of three indefinite Hebrew time words. He chose the only word that means a literal day, and the Jews understood it literally (until the idea of millions of years developed in the early nineteenth century). For this reason, the day-age view or framework hypothesis must be rejected. The gap theory or any other attempt to put millions of years before the six days are also false because God says that in six days He made the heaven and the earth and the sea and *all* that is in them. So He made everything in those six literal days and nothing before the first day.

5. **Noah's Flood washes away millions of years.** The evidence in Genesis 6–9 for a global catastrophic flood is overwhelming. For example, the Flood was intended to destroy not only all sinful people but also all land animals and birds and the surface of the earth, which only a global flood could accomplish. The Ark's purpose was to save two of every kind of land animal and bird (and seven of some) to repopulate the earth after the Flood. The Ark was totally unnecessary if the Flood was only local. People, animals, and birds could have migrated out of the flood zone before it occurred, or the zone could have been populated from creatures outside the area after the Flood. The catastrophic nature of the Flood is seen in the nonstop rain for at least 40 days, which would have produced massive erosion, mud slides, hurricanes, etc. The Hebrew words translated "the fountains of the great deep burst open" (Genesis 7:11) clearly point to tectonic rupturing of the earth's surface in many places for 150 days, resulting in volcanoes, earthquakes, and tsunamis. Noah's Flood would produce exactly the kind of complex geological record we see worldwide today: thousands of feet of sediments clearly deposited by water and later hardened into rock and containing billions of fossils. If the year-long Flood is responsible for most of the rock layers and fossils, then those rocks and fossils cannot represent the history of the earth over millions of years, as evolutionists claim.

6. **Jesus was a young-earth creationist.** Jesus consistently treated the miracle accounts of the Old Testament as straightforward, truthful, historical accounts (e.g., creation of Adam, Noah and the Flood, Lot and his wife in Sodom, Moses and the manna, and Jonah in the fish). He continually affirmed the authority of Scripture over men's ideas and traditions (Matthew 15:1–9). In Mark 10:6 we have the clearest (but not the only) statement showing that Jesus was a young-earth creationist. He teaches that Adam and Eve were made at the "*beginning* of creation,"

not billions of years after the beginning, as would be the case if the universe were really billions of years old. So, if Jesus was a young-earth creationist, then how can His faithful followers have any other view?

7. **Belief in millions of years undermines the Bible's teaching on death and on the character of God.** Genesis 1 says six times that God called the creation "good," and when He finished creation on Day 6, He called everything "very good." Man and animals and birds were originally vegetarian (Genesis 1:29–30, plants are not "living creatures," as people and animals are, according to Scripture). But Adam and Eve sinned, resulting in the judgment of God on the whole creation. Instantly Adam and Eve died spiritually, and after God's curse they began to die physically. The serpent and Eve were changed physically and the ground itself was cursed (Genesis 3:14–19). The whole creation now groans in bondage to corruption, waiting for the final redemption of Christians (Romans 8:19–25) when we will see the restoration of all things (Acts 3:21, Colossians 1:20) to a state

similar to the pre-Fall world, when there will be no more carnivorous behavior (Isaiah 11:6–9) and no disease, suffering, or death (Revelation 21:3–5) because there will be no more Curse (Revelation 22:3). To accept millions of years of animal death before the creation and Fall of man contradicts and destroys the Bible's teaching on death and the full redemptive work of Christ. It also makes God into a bumbling, cruel creator who uses (or can't prevent) disease, natural disasters, and extinctions to mar His creative work, without any moral cause, but still calls it all "very good."

8. **The idea of millions of years did not come from the scientific facts.** This idea of long ages was developed by deistic and atheistic geologists in the late eighteenth and early nineteenth centuries. These men used antibiblical philosophical and religious assumptions to interpret the geological observations in a way that plainly contradicted the biblical account of creation, the Flood, and the age of the earth. Most church leaders and scholars quickly compromised using the gap theory, day-age view, local flood view, etc. to try to fit "deep time" into the Bible. But they did not understand the geological arguments, and they did not defend their views by careful Bible study. The "deep time" idea flows out of naturalistic assumptions, not scientific observations.

9. **Radiometric dating methods do not prove millions of years.** Radiometric dating was not developed until the early twentieth century, by which time virtually the whole world had already accepted the millions of years. For many years creation scientists have cited numerous examples in the published scientific literature of these dating methods clearly giving erroneous dates (e.g., a date of millions of years for lava flows that occurred in the past few hundred years or even decades). In recent years creationists in the RATE project have done

experimental, theoretical, and field research to uncover more such evidence (e.g., diamonds and coal, which the evolutionists say are millions of years old, were dated by carbon-14 to be only thousands of years old) and to show that decay rates were orders of magnitude faster in the past, which shrinks the millions of years to thousands of years, confirming the Bible.[1]

Conclusion

These are just some of the reasons why we believe that the Bible is giving us the true history of the world. God's Word must be the final authority on all matters about which it speaks—not just the moral and spiritual matters, but also its teachings that bear on history, archaeology, and science.

What is at stake here is the authority of Scripture, the character of God, the doctrine of death, and the very foundation of the gospel. If the early chapters of Genesis are not true literal history, then faith in the rest of the Bible is undermined, including its teaching about salvation and morality. I urge you to carefully read the other chapters in this book. The health of the church, the effectiveness of her mission to a lost world, and the glory of God are at stake.

1.   For the results of the RATE project, see Larry Vardiman, Andrew Snelling, and Eugene Chaffin, eds., *Radioisitopes and the Age of the Earth*, Vol. 2 (Master Books, 2005); and Don DeYoung, *Thousands ... Not Billions* (Master Books, 2005).

The Good News

You may have heard the word gospel used in different ways. Someone may claim the story they are telling you is the "gospel truth," or you may hear of a gospel quartet coming to the local music hall. But what does that word mean and where did it come from?

In Greek culture, heralds were sent on behalf of generals or kings to announce the news. The word in Greek for "good news" is where the word evangelism comes from. When Christians evangelize, they are spreading the good news of the gospel. But in order to have good news, there must be some bad news.

The bad news goes back thousands of years to a time when God had created a perfect universe. There was no death, suffering, or disease, and the first people, Adam and Eve, obeyed God perfectly. Then it all changed. They broke God's command and sin entered into the world. That sin broke the relationship between man and God and has infected all of humanity—even you.

If you stop and analyze your life in light of what the Bible reveals about God's commands to His creatures, you will realize that sin is part of your life. The essence of the commands of God are summed up by Jesus when He said, "You shall love the Lord your God with all your heart, with all your soul, and with all your mind. This is the first and great commandment. And the second is like it: You shall love your neighbor as yourself" (Matthew 22:37–39).

Have you?

The Bible makes the claim that all men have fallen short of this standard (Romans 3:9–23). To reject this authority is like telling a judge you don't believe he can enforce the speeding law you are accused of breaking. But there is a difference, God is a perfectly just judge and His punishment is eternal (Psalm 7:11). If you die having committed even a single sin against God, you face that judgment (Hebrews 9:27).

But there is good news! God is also merciful and gracious, and He has provided a way of escape for sinners. Jesus Christ, who is God in the flesh, stepped into this corrupted world, lived a life of perfect obedience, took the wrath of God against sin upon Himself as He died on the Cross, and was raised to life. All of those who turn from their sins and place their trust in Jesus have their record wiped clean—all their debts paid—and the perfect record of Jesus applied to their account. God has provided a great exchange—your sin for the righteousness of Jesus—and that goodness should bring you to call upon His mercy (Romans 2:1–16).